Dear Real Estate Agent,

There Are Answers.

Six Industry Professionals Share Their Knowledge

Katherine Scarim
Gregory R. Cohen, Esquire
Gerald Pumphrey
Guy Hartman
Mark Shanz
Kelly Sturmthal, Esq.

Table of Contents

HOME INSPECTION

INSURANCE

BUSINESS LAW

OUR CONCLUSION, YOUR BEGINNING

PREFACE

Alone we can do so little;
together we can do so much.

- Helen Keller

Too many real estate agents wrongly believe their success is solely a result of their actions. Nothing could be further from the truth. As an agent, your success *is highly dependent* on other skilled and knowledgeable real estate related professionals. The best agents not only make certain to hone their skills and increase their knowledge on a daily basis, but they *also* surround themselves with a core group of "go-to" professionals who are equally dedicated to excelling in their fields. A real estate agent's core group typically consists of at least one of each of the following:

- Real Estate Attorney
- Home Inspector
- Mortgage Broker
- Insurance Broker
- Business Attorney

Always be looking for the right professionals to add to your core group.

Weak agents fumble through deal after deal with subpar related professionals selected by the other side.

Strong agents have expert related professionals to recommend to their clients. When they work deals, they know their core group is working just as hard as they are to efficiently and legally close the deal. Moreover, these experts provide the agent peace of mind that their clients are being treated with the amount of care and respect they deserve. Strong agents will always refer clients to their core group.

Specific deals aside, *both* the real estate agent's and the related professionals' *businesses as a whole* should benefit exponentially from their relationships, which must be built on mutual trust and respect. Such relationships prove beneficial when:

- Individuals make themselves available to answer one another's questions.

- Individuals share newly obtained industry-specific knowledge that they believe might impact the others' businesses.

- Individuals share networking invitations.

- Individuals share related business opportunities (the writing of this book for example).

- Individuals refer business to one another.

The most obvious benefit, "referring business to one another," is often the most misunderstood. Its placement as the last item on the list is intentional. Receiving business *should not* be the agent's foremost determining factor as to who to include in their core group. However over time, it should be the natural result of nurturing such relationships.

Professionals should be selected based on skill, knowledge, integrity, and client interactions.

That said, professionals must also be vetted to ascertain that they have the business savvy to understand that the agent can only feed their businesses as long as the agent has business themselves.

Most likely, the better attorneys and mortgage brokers have years in the industry and therefore already have referral relationships. That is to be expected. However, they also have the largest numbers of referrals to give. Overtime, if they do in fact trust and value your contributions to the relationship, referrals should result.

Insurance brokers and home inspectors are rarely contacted before clients have a real estate agent. However, they are still members of the community and have friends and family that buy and sell real estate. When they know that you are working hard to better their business, there is no reason why they cannot be referring you to their personal sphere.

Becoming an excellent agent does not happen overnight, nor does forming your core group. Every now and then, you will come across a real estate related professional that exceeds both your and your clients' expectations. That's when the magic starts to happen…

Dear Real Estate Agent,

We got ourselves into one hell of a business didn't we?

Regardless of how the public might view us, you and I both know we've thrown our hat in the ring of one of the most competitive industries out there. No one can imagine what it's truly like to be a real estate agent until they have been in the trenches.

We wake up every day and push through rejection after rejection, clean up other agents' sloppy contract work, place phone call after email after text to unresponsive brokers, loan officers, and title officers… and here's the kicker, we don't always get paid, even when we do an amazing job for our clients.

Financing doesn't come through, clear title is not attainable, repair costs are too high, sellers are unrealistic – and so we smile. We smile and tell our clients, "Don't worry, it happens. This one was not meant to be. We'll find you another home (or other buyers)."

But it does matter. We will *never* be compensated for those hours. Yet we pull ourselves up from our bootstraps and do it again.

Why?

I can only come up with one answer. We remain in this crazy wonderful business because we crave variety and get some sort of sick high off the never-ending challenge. You never know what is going to come at you; you never fail to learn something new every day.

Property transactions are like snowflakes – each one different and perfectly imperfect.

The only black and white that exists in our world is the ink on our contracts; we swim in a sea of gray, often against the current.

We spend our days performing the near impossible. Staying on top of all the parties' responsibilities while keeping everyone's emotions in check and making certain they meet deadlines. I liken it to herding cats.

Oh yeah, and we like the big commission checks.

Admit it. Holding a $15,000 check in your hand with your name on it, even if it truly reflects having made only $3.20/hour on a yearlong home search, *feels awesome*. We hold that gorgeous babe in our hands after nine months of house hunting misery and 24 hours of the most excruciating closing process and all of the sudden – it was all worth it. Just like a new mom, we too forget about all the horrors that allowed us that amazing and precious reward – and we can't wait to do it again, and again, and again! Someone should create transaction control pills...

Sarcasm aside, I'm proud to call myself a real estate broker. I take great pride in professionally representing and protecting my clients through their real estate transactions. I also find incredible reward in supporting my associates and helping them navigate their transactions. I deeply believe we provide an important service to our clients, and that our clients are better off for having our expertise to help guide them.

I dream of the day that states mandate contract coursework and mentoring for new licensees. Such a requirement would hopefully stop having agents "fake it 'til they make it" on the unsuspecting public, and tarnishing the reputation of our industry. Unfortunately, agents are not required to join the National Association of REALTORS®, which has carefully constructed the Code of Ethics and Standards of Professionalism for REALTORS® to adhere to.

In the meantime, I will try to better help our industry a bit by writing books for those agents, REALTORS® or not, who strive to learn as much as possible – so they are better prepared to navigate their clients through the choppy waters of real estate.

Sincerely,

Katherine Scarim
Broker/Owner
Island Bridge Realty

WHAT WE ACTUALLY SELL

As a real estate agent, I believe you are in the business of selling two products, *Positive Relationships* and *Clean Contract Work*. These are the foundation of every real estate transaction. The home itself that conveys as a result is tertiary.

Should the relationship with our clients fail, contract work will be scrutinized and any flaw or omission will be brought to light and pursued, possibly through litigation. On the other hand, should we fail to protect our clients through clean contract work, we have set the relationship on a path to dissolution.

Positive Relationships and *Clean Contract Work* – one can't happen without the other...

CLIENT RELATIONS

Unfortunately, most real estate agents do not join our industry having obtained a masters in psychology. Therefore, the majority of agents will have to struggle along without complete understanding of how the human mind works and the resulting human behaviors. The best that agents can do is to be as mindful as possible when navigating through their relationships with clients.

Clients need to be heard.

Clients that lean toward logic-based thinking will need to have their *reasoning* for their thoughts and actions heard. Even if you don't agree with their reasoning, listen and acknowledge it in the most positive light possible. Afterwards, your opinion/advice is more likely to be entertained. If you find yourself feeling you need to "win" or "tell them like it is" during your exchanges with clients, you should immediately step back and re-evaluate how you are interacting.

Clients who lean towards emotional thoughts will need to have their *feelings* heard. Make time to listen. Accept that a client's feelings, while intangible, are a highly influential party in the transaction. Sometimes just having you, their agent, acknowledge that they are frustrated with the selling, buying, or leasing process is enough. Don't automatically throw logical solutions at them – they may not want solutions, just a sounding board. Should they believe their feelings are being dismissed, they often respond by either lashing out or shutting down communication (both of which would prove disastrous).

Be honest with yourself about the type of thinking you fall into most. Should you be more logic-based, be especially cautious when dealing with emotion-based clients; your instinctual response is likely to be wrong. The same is true if you're an emotion-based thinker dealing with logic-based clients.

Know when to ask for help.

At the first sign of a client relationship heading south, consider reaching out for help. There will be a point of deterioration where no one will be able to salvage the situation – do not let it get there before you ask for help.

Hopefully, you are under a broker who is happy to talk through any situation with you. If you both believe it to be beneficial, be willing to speak with your clients directly. The broker may consider having another agent complete the contract for you, if you and/or the clients so wish. Moreover, if clients are refusing your advice/recommendations on a legal/contractual matter which could prove detrimental to them, or they fail to meet their contractual obligations, your broker can help decide if reaching out to an attorney would be warranted.

Keep in mind, no matter how supportive and available your broker is to you, he/she is of little use "after the fact." Once any party signs something questionable, or once communications have broken down, the likelihood for a broker to be able to step in and solve a situation is at best greatly diminished, or worse, impossible.

Trust your gut and always follow through.

Do not override your gut feeling of not being able to work well with someone just to make a sale. When considering who to take on as a client, be honest with yourself as to whether or not their personality and needs are what you can comfortably work with. If there is just "something about them" that you are not comfortable with, refer them out. The right agent exists for every client. Save your sanity, make a partial commission, and remove all liability by referring such clients to an agent that would work better with them than yourself.

Moreover, if you have had a difficult or unpleasant experience with a client in the past, do not make the mistake of relegating that experience to a specific property. The next property is just that, another property. However, the client's lack of respect for you, stubbornness, disregard for the law, etc. will follow you to each new property. Addresses change, but personalities don't; *refer the client out.*

Should you realize that you failed to listen to your instincts and are now in an uncomfortable situation with a client, you will need to follow it through if you are already in a contractual relationship with obligations. Listen carefully for what the client needs to be heard, and reach out for help as discussed above. Do not allow yourself to grow frustrated and let communications become volatile or silent.

A relationship is two-sided, set expectations for both parties.

An important concept to keep in mind – clients are different from headaches.

Headaches don't respect your time, and they view you as replaceable. You will know a headache when you meet one. They refuse to get pre-qualified, try to pit you against other agents, and don't respond to your communications yet expect you to drop everything immediately when they want to see a home. You do not want headaches.

Clients, on the other hand, value your time and knowledge. They are grateful that you are honest and professional. Better yet, clients recommend you to other clients.

How do you weed out headaches and keep clients from turning into headaches? Ask if your brokerage provides a Client/Agent Communications

Expectations form. (If they don't, you should create one for yourself.) This form should determine preferred methods of communications (call, email, text), working hours, how long to expect a return communication, etc. upfront. It can be submitted to your clients to complete or simply used as a conversation template.

Setting communication expectations upfront does more than determine how late is too late to call, it actually sets the tone for your future agent/client relationship. Remember, you don't want headaches. You want clients. Having them acknowledge how and when you work reinforces you are a professional and expect to be treated as such. You will not jump when they say jump. You are running a business, and while they are important to you, they are one of many clients you will be servicing. Once the terms are agreed upon, follow through and meet, or better yet exceed, their expectations.

The one question that you must ask EVERY client.

Before you leave the listing appointment. *Before* you start showing prospective buyers' and tenants' homes. If you never implement another suggestion from this book, please for the sake of your business and your future in real estate as a whole, ask the following of each and every client:

"Do I have your permission to be honest with you?"

Memorize that simple question – and *always* ask it.

"Do I have your permission to be honest with you?"

Why? Because when asked such a loaded question, the client has no possible response other than, "Yes, of course." And that simple yes is pure gold.

Calmly respond with, "That's so good to hear Mr. Seller/Buyer, because unfortunately I find some clients only want to be told what they want to hear whether or not it's the truth, and that often derails my ability to help them accomplish what they hired me for – to get their home sold/find them a home that's right for them. Now that I know

you are committed to approaching the sale/purchase of your home from a logical, as opposed to emotional, standpoint, I am confident that we will have a successful outcome."
Say nothing more; change the topic.

At some point during every transaction, one or more of your clients will become emotional. We typically see heightened emotions during the offer stage, repair negotiations, or after a low appraisal.

Once you start to feel your client is leaning away from logic, you can reel them back in by calmly and quietly saying, "Mr. Seller, do you remember back when we first started working together and you assured me that I had your permission to always tell you the truth? I understand that you may be feeling _____ right now. However, I feel compelled to tell you _____ and that, in my experience, the logical response in this situation would be _____. Is there a chance you could try to step outside your emotions for a minute and look at the bigger picture so we are certain that you are not reacting stronger today than you might if you were not emotionally bogged down in the heat of the moment?"

Emotional clients kill deals and initiate lawsuits. *Calming clients is one of the most important skills a real estate agent can learn.*

Protect yourself during communications with clients.

Beyond the obvious that all communications should be professional in nature, you should take the following precautions to limit liability for you and the brokerage firm:

1. Emails

At minimum, you should include in your email signature (on all your devices):

- Full name
- Brokerage name
- Your phone number
- Brokerage address

And the following (or similar) disclaimers:

- E-mails sent or received shall neither constitute acceptance of conducting transactions via electronic means nor create a binding contract until and unless a written contract is signed by all parties.

- This e-mail transmission, any links contained within and/or attachments may be confidential. If you are not the intended recipient, you are hereby notified that any disclosure, copying, distribution, or use of the information contained herein is strictly prohibited. If you have received this e-mail transmission in error, please notify the sender and then immediately delete it.

Make certain to save *all* e-mails grouped by transaction for future reference, for a minimum of five years; save them for seven years should there be a legal investigation pending. Emails of great importance should be forwarded to your brokerage to be kept with their files.

Set up and utilize a mail tracking software such as MailTracker.io (for Gmail users). Receiving notification when your emails are read not only gives you peace of mind during your transaction, but in situations when time is of the essence, or you require proof of disclosure, cancellations, etc., the read receipt will become a record of value to attach to the file.

Check your state's licensing laws for any additional signature items or disclosures that may be required and number of years to keep correspondences on file.

2. Texts

While texting is a way of life, be conscious about what should and should not be sent via text. Never intentionally engage in an important conversation via text. However, should you find yourself in a situation where you would need to save a text for your file, do one of the following:

- Screenshot the text conversation and email to yourself.

- Re-type the text into an email and send to the other party to acknowledge its content.

- Purchase a data backup app to store texts, voicemails, etc.

3. Voice Mail

At minimum, your full name, your brokerage's name, and a statement of thanks should be within your voicemail message. Ideally your voicemail should be updated daily and also include the current date, a loose recount of your schedule, and a gauge as to when the caller can expect their call to be returned.

> "You have reached Katherine Scarim, broker/owner of Island Bridge Realty. Today is April 23rd, and I will be in meetings from 12-2 p.m. I will return all calls thereafter. Thank you for calling and have a great day!"

This daily message works two-fold; it alleviates the clients' fear that you are not checking calls or not getting back to them soon enough, and it reinforces that you are a busy professional who works on a schedule – not on your clients' every whim.

4. Postal Mail

Should you need to mail something of significant importance to clients, send *two*:

The first, "Return Receipt Requested" so you have the return signature card on file.

At the same time, send an identical copy via regular mail, so that if they refuse to sign the signature card of the first (so they can state "they never read it") you can refute that it was also sent via postal mail in a legal situation.

CONTRACT WORK

To be an agent of value, you must give contract work the importance it deserves. Almost daily, an associate will show me yet another offer (or contract) submitted by a cooperating agent that either has conflicting dates and terms, is incomplete, or fails to protect their clients in one scenario or another.

Learning Contracts

Every real estate agent must acquire and maintain a strong understanding of their state contracts, disclosures, riders, and addendum. This is no easy task, as laws and therefore contracts are constantly changing.

Moreover, no two deals are ever the same.

If a contract is not properly drafted, your clients, your license, and the deal are all in jeopardy.

Ideally, all agents could reduce their liability by having an attorney draft all contract work. However, the reality is in many scenarios this is not possible. For example, some clients may not be willing to pay for an attorney's services. Other times, multiple offer scenarios require a contract be drafted late at night or on a weekend when an attorney is not available.

While it might be the least glamorous part of real estate, contract drafting is, by far, the most important facet to consider. You must become proficient working within standard contracts and weaving in additional forms to accomplish each clients' unique objectives.

You have no right *ethically or legally* to ask clients to sign a document you don't understand. Always explain what the clients are signing, and make certain if you don't know an answer to one of their questions, that you get it answered *before* they sign.

Set aside a portion of your day, every day*, until you have a full understanding* of each Contract, Addendum, Rider, and Disclosure utilized by your state and brokerage office. If you are short on time, I personally give you permission to stop prospecting for clients (gasp!) and direct your energies for several days towards learning contracts. You do not deserve clients if you are unwilling to take the time to learn how to protect them contractually. Period.

1. First, read the document as a whole for general comprehension.

What is the purpose of the form? When would it be used?

Does it stand on its own or complement another contract?

Is it legally required or intended as an added layer of protection?

Who is required to sign or initial the form?

2. Next, read the document line by line.

What does the form require to be filled in? If there are blank lines, what are the corresponding default amounts or terms, if any? Why were those default amounts likely chosen? Highlight any blanks on the document.

Does any wording read vaguely? Underline "gray" areas of the form.

Are options given for you to select? Write next to each option what you believe would be the ramifications of choosing it.

Would selecting any option on this form trigger completing an additional document? Write which document you believe you would need on the bottom of the form or staple the secondary document to it.

Would failing to perform any specific action result in default of the contract? Is there a determined time frame in which the action must be performed? What monies or rights would be forfeited as a result?

Scrawl questions in the margins as you think of them.

Get your questions answered.

Bring all you marked up forms to either your:

- real estate attorney
- broker
- broker assigned mentor
- REALTOR® Board contracts class

Be persistent in getting your questions answered.

If you still have a few lingering questions, or ones that you didn't think of until later, and you are a REALTOR®, you can call your free state REALTOR® legal hotline and ask for a few minutes of their time.

Writing Offers

Armed with an understanding of the contracts you will be using, you are now in a position to protect yourself and your clients assuming you always:

Take Your Time

Real Estate associates, especially new associates, often feel pressure to produce offers and other paperwork at alarming speed. Whether it is market driven (multiple offer scenarios) or client driven (anxious first-time buyers or busy corporate clients) associates often work faster than prudence calls for.

Slow down.

Control your product.

Do not allow your clients, license, or deal to be jeopardized. No judge or mediator reviewing a complaint filed against you will ever accept, "I was trying to hurry for my client," or, "We were going to lose the house to another bidder," as an acceptable defense for your negligence.

Slow down.

Dot Your I's and Cross Your T's

1. Fill in *every* blank.

This simple habit leaves no room for post-signing additions or arguments that the contract is unenforceable due to an omission of a key term.

If there is a default clause after the blank, for example, "15 days if left blank," still fill in "15" if you are in agreement with the default amount.

If the blank is a line for a monetary or percentage amount that is not a factor in your deal, still write in "0.00" or "zero" or "———."

If blank lines are present for wording to be inserted and you don't need to fill them in, simply write "None" or "N/A."

2. Obtain information from the *correct* source.

A Multiple Listing Service (MLS) listing is *not* a source of information that you can rely on entirely.

Property owners' names should be checked against the deed, which are easily accessible online in the County Clerk's public records. Should you find record of someone owning the property other than who the agent represents, get that agent on the phone and get to the bottom of it. Possible scenarios that could be the cause:

- The home recently changed ownership and the new deed has yet to be recorded.

- The agent incorrectly named a party with Power of Attorney over the sale as the owner.

- Someone is fraudulently trying to sell the property and the other agent is unaware.

Should the owner be married, but the spouse does not appear on the deed, it would be wise to speak to an attorney or title company to learn if your state requires they be included on the contract.

While reviewing the deed, also obtain the Legal Description for the property.

Check the Property Identification Number(s) (PIN#s) against the tax records. One would expect to be able to search property tax records by address or owner name on the County Appraiser's site.

Confirm financing terms with buyers' lender. The contract will be contingent upon financing being obtained according to the terms within.

Do not commit your client to financing terms you have not confirmed as accurate with their lender. Occasionally terms are spelled out on the Pre-Approval letter provided by the lender. If not, call or email your buyers' lender to confirm the following:

- Amount to be financed
- Loan product being used (Conventional, FHA, VA)
- Financing percentage cap
- Length of loan (15 year, 30 year)
- Number of days needed for loan approval
- Minimum amount of days to get clear to close

3. Make certain *every* item your clients expect to convey with the home is written on the contract or an attachment.

Technology is your friend in this matter. Once your clients show interest in a home, photograph or video tape any items owned by the sellers that exist on the property and your clients expect to convey.

Refer to your photos when drafting the contract. Be specific as to the number and type of items. "Pool equipment" is vague. "Gas pool heater, pump, and skimmer," leaves little room for confusion. When items of significant expense or importance to your clients are to be conveyed, be as detailed in your wording as possible. "Hurricane shutters" is vague. "Steel panel hurricane shutters and associated hardware fitting the home's 32 windows and two doors" is specific. Reference and attach copies of the photos to the contract if a unique situation warrants.

Maintain copies of the photos or video in your electronic files. Should your contract have a list of default items that convey with the home, be certain to strike through items that do not exist on the property.

If you learn through the listing broker or the MLS that the sellers are NOT conveying certain items, make certain those items are clearly removed from conveyance on the contract.

4. **Make certain *every* addendum, rider, and disclosure that should be part of the contract is attached to the offer.**

As you draw up the offer, make certain to include all addendum and disclosures that are triggered by your offer terms or property characteristics. As of this writing, Florida REALTORS® had three riders, 17 disclosures, and 39 addendums available in their forms library. Be thoughtful in your selection.

Even if your clients are not required to sign an addendum until the other party discloses certain items listed on it, you should still make certain the contract references the addendum and send the unsigned addendum with the offer. This assures that it will not be overlooked, and that it will be included within the final bilaterally signed contract.

5. **And then there is the completely blank "Addendum to Contract."**

A blank addendum should **only** be used to accommodate situations that arise outside the scope of the existing forms.

If legal in your state, and you find yourself having to draft verbiage for a clear cut, deal-specific situation, use the blank addendum. However, be cautious with your wording, and never be vague. Slow down and think of all the possible misunderstandings or problems that could result, and choose words that address those issues.

Let's work through an example. Your clients want the sellers to agree to remove a built-in shelving unit from the property. The typical agent will quickly write up the addendum exactly to that affect:

"Sellers agree to remove the built-in shelving unit from the Property."

It's what the clients wanted. But does it protect them properly?

After some thought, you will realize your clients are not just asking you to make sure the unit is gone, but also that the property not be damaged in the process and that it is removed in a timely manner. The above wording does not protect your clients from unscrupulous sellers who might rip it out of the wall on the way to the closing, leaving a mess behind.

A strong, well thought out addendum will read:

"Sellers and buyers agree, at the sellers' expense the built-in shelving unit in the master bedroom is to be removed from the property and the wall it was attached to be patched and painted so no visible evidence remains. Work to be completed no later than three (3) days prior to closing."

Much better.

However, if the deal requires a complicated, expensive, and/or legal issue to be addressed using a blank addendum, protect your clients and reduce your liability by having a real estate attorney write it. At minimum, draft the verbiage to the best of your ability and then have a real estate attorney review and clean it *prior* to having any party sign. Do not fall into a situation where you could be accused of practicing law without a license.

NON-TRANSACTIONAL CONTRACTS

Standard contracts aside, I have two non-transaction related contracts I want you to thoughtfully write and revise on occasion. Neither will jeopardize your license, nor bring about litigation should you improperly draft them. However, failing to give them the weight they deserve could cost you your business and/or family – so take heed.

Personal Protection Order

A personal protection order is, in essence, a restraining order keeping real estate from harassing and endangering your family and sanity. Those of you who have been in the industry any length of time know just how important, and extremely difficult, it is to keep real estate from taking over every minute of your life. If you are new to the business, you might think I'm being overdramatic. I'm not. If you become passionate about real estate, and that internal fire to succeed gets lit, you will be consumed by it.

Moreover there is some peculiar badge of honor in our industry to say we work 24/7. New agents fear missing "the unicorn call" – the mythical career changing lead *that might go to another agent* if they aren't at the ready. Established agents fear not sounding busy; the public might assume they aren't any good if there isn't a phone attached to their ear during every one of their kids' sporting or school events. I've been guilty of both. Most agents are. But you can do better.

Your personal protective order should be written with the provision that real estate clients, functions, duties, etc. may not encroach on certain dates and times. Make certain vacations are scheduled and included. Your personal protective order is your best chance at maintaining any resemblance of a work/life balance. If you have a significant other or children, make certain that they are included in choosing the dates and times to protect. Better yet, have them sign it with the obligation that they must hold you accountable, perhaps with a predetermined fine or "punishment" to keep you in check.

During your first year in real estate, with its huge learning curve and no pipeline or referral base to draw from, you will need to have your family's understanding that your protected time and dates might be only one sacred night a week. However, as you get a grasp on the industry, you owe it to yourself and your family to streamline your business, to work smart, not hard. Revisit your protective order every now and then to carve out additional real estate free hours or days your loved ones can count on.

Advertising Dollars Contract

Marketing is an important piece of the real estate puzzle, and limited, *strategic* marketing is necessary. Due to the volumes of books, blogs, professional marketers, and real estate coaches solely devoted to assisting you with marketing, I will avoid specifics regarding *how to* advertise. However, I am compelled to say blindly spending advertising dollars is a treacherous road many new and established agents go down. This unharnessed spending is without a doubt one major contributing factor as to why so many agents are forced to leave the industry.

Save your business by writing and upholding a contract with yourself as to what your advertising dollars may be spent on and the most you will spend on a given campaign. Decide at the beginning a date for cancellation should the campaign not produce the results you require. Track and measure *all* your advertising, *always*, to determine if it is producing a positive return on your investment (ROI) or not. When you mail out $3,000 worth of postcards, you need to earn $3,000 as a direct result of the mailing to break even. Should the mailing result in earning more than $3,000 in commissions, the ad produced a positive ROI; less than $3,000 would result in a negative ROI. Low-performing ads will need to be revisited and tweaked before rerunning to avoid throwing more good money at poor investments. Rinse and repeat until you have an ad that is consistently producing results. As ads are never perfect the first time, I strongly suggest controlling your advertising dollars by only committing small amounts during the testing phase of new campaigns. Once your ads are leading prospects to reach out to you and begin resulting in closed sales, allot more of your advertising dollars to the proven campaign.

I once heard, "If you want to make money in real estate, sell *to* real estate agents." I wish I knew who said this, because they absolutely deserve recognition for so cleanly stating such a poignant truth.

Try to think from an advertising representative's perspective. It does not matter what they are selling; it could be postcards, logo shirts, or internet ads. Think about what a cash cow of a demographic real estate agents are. According to the National Association of REALTORS® (NAR), we have the *largest* trade association in the United States, with *over a million* members. If that number seems high, consider that not every real estate agent is a member of NAR! On top of that, our industry is a bit of a revolving door – with new agents coming in as fast as others leave. Each new agent needs to advertise and let the world know they are now selling real estate. Even established agents are excellent targets. Many tend to be transient in business. Guess what that means? Every time they change brokerages, they need new signs, new announcement postcards, etc.

Now factor in that paid advertising is a form of passive prospecting. This means it requires little discomfort on the part of the agent as opposed to actually putting themselves out there in the community by knocking on doors, networking, and holding open houses – all which come with the possibility of dreaded face to face rejections. Real estate agents, even though they may intellectually know better, will always hope for positive results through passive advertisements, and therefore find some way, any way, to justify paying for advertising. Anything to avoid the uncomfortable (yet proven) methods of active prospecting. Do not think for a second that the advertisers don't know this. How often have your read ads that start with, "Never make a cold call again!" or "Quit open houses for good!"

Don't be a fool. Override your fears, be careful with your money, and save your business.

There is no right or wrong way to draft your advertising dollars contract, just make certain you *hold yourself to it*. Better yet, share your contract with a spouse or co-worker and ask them to help hold you accountable.

- Set a future date to review and, if necessary, revise the contract at no earlier than six months and no longer than a year.

- If you are a new agent, or just switched brokerages, have a separate, fixed amount determined for your basic marketing necessities (business cards, website, and yard signs).

- Determine how much to spend per ad and/or campaign while in the testing phase and represent it as either a fixed dollar amount *or* an amount based on a percentage. For example, costs will not exceed $2,000 a year, or 10% of my commissions for the next six months.

No matter what terms you set, adhere to them until your next scheduled review or you have an ad campaign that is consistently returning a positive ROI worth putting additional monies into.

OBTAINING KNOWLEDGE

Without question, the Achilles heel of the real estate industry is how little knowledge many agents possess. Partially at blame may be that our industry somewhat prides itself on having such a low bar for entry.

In the true spirit of the American dream, any of us can rise to riches if we are just willing to work hard enough. Licensing tests can be taken, taken again, and retaken indefinitely; the prior education requirement is only a high school diploma. And you know what? I actually agree with everyone having a chance to make it in our industry. We should not block hardworking, talented people from making a great living in this country.

What I don't agree with is allowing newly licensed (and sadly too many not-so-newly licensed) agents to practice real estate on the unsuspecting public without a solid foundation of contract knowledge, a working understanding of legal, insurance, mortgage, and inspection issues, nor mandated mentoring during their first several transactions. To date, *the burden of acquiring such an education lies squarely on the shoulders of the individual agent/brokers.*

Superlative brokerages will make certain every agent is provided a proper education, through in-house and/or outsourced classes, seminars, and assigned mentoring.

However, some brokerages scramble to get the agent in the field as fast as possible, bulking them up with training comprised mostly of how to market and obtain leads, yet little more. They would argue that if a new agent doesn't start generating income immediately, they will quickly grow discouraged and quit, and that it is best to learn as you go. Personally, I believe this to be short sighted; it opens the brokerage and agent to liability, and simultaneously diminishes the likelihood of long-term success.

To provide value and be able to protect your clients, you must accept that it is *your first and foremost duty* to seek out classes, seminars, and experiences while developing a network of knowledgeable professionals to learn from in order to acquire a high level of competency.

Also, keep in mind that our industry is always changing. The only way to *stay* proficient is to continue to pursue educational opportunities for the entirety of your career.

Attend Classes

There are Bachelors and Masters degree programs for Real Estate should you wish to pursue the bulk of your education in a structured setting.

However, if you are like most agents, you will choose to self-direct your education. You must challenge yourself to fill in foundational knowledge gaps, keep abreast of changes, and seek out niche information that lends itself directly to your clients' needs. Be thoughtful and strategic about where you choose to spend your time and money. Different opportunities include:

- **Local REALTORS® Board Classes**

  Your local REALTORS® board most likely provides numerous classes every month. They are often free; rarely are they cost prohibitive. Common topics are new contract reviews, MLS training, ethics, various financing options, legal seminars, and niche classes (seniors, military relocation, Section 8, etc.). If you have more than one board in your area, ask if the other board(s) allow non-members to attend their classes for a fee. If so, ask to be put on the list for notification of upcoming classes.

  If you find yourself impressed by a speaker or instructor, introduce yourself during a break. After leaving, connect on social media or send an email complimenting them on their presentation and offer to take them for coffee. *Always pursue quality individuals to include in your professional sphere.*

- **National Association of REALTORS® Designations and Certifications**

  NAR and its affiliates design coursework and reward designations and certifications to REALTORS® who complete it. Some accreditations also require experiential hours. Courses are typically taught at local boards or online. The designations and certifications provide you with industry approved instruction, a network of former graduates, and the ability to market your achievement through use of the associated acronym after your name and provided logo.

- **Related Industries' Seminars and Conferences**

  Always stay mindful that, as a real estate agent, *you are the generalist in a transaction dependent on specialists.* Clients expect you to be able to answer general questions and problem solve common scenarios regarding insurance, financing, real estate law, title, and inspections. Never pass up an opportunity to attend a lecture or conference designed for insurance brokers, home inspectors, title officers, mortgage brokers, or real estate attorneys. Attending such events benefits you two-fold.

    1. You acquire information other agents are unlikely to be presented through basic real estate channels.

    2. You are given the opportunity to network with related industry professionals, who simply by being in attendance, have demonstrated their commitment to stay abreast of their industry. These are precisely the type of professionals you want to rely on for advice and recommend to your clients.

- **State Licensing Agency**

  Always strive to acquire the highest level of licensing your state offers. In Florida, we have two tiers, the initial Sales Associate license and the higher Broker's license. After a minimum number of years, licensed Sales Associates can, with additional coursework and testing, obtain a Broker's license. Should they continue to hang their Broker's license under another Broker, they are referred to as Broker Associates. However, if they wish to open their own brokerage, the Broker's license allows them to do so.

  I often ask Sales Associates who have been in the business a while why they have not acquired their Broker's license. The two most common responses are, "Why bother?" and, "I don't want the additional liability."

Why bother? Because you owe it to your clients and your business to obtain the highest level of education and licensing your state allows. Why would you settle with being one of many when you have the chance to be one of few? Why wouldn't you want the higher status to include on your business cards and marketing materials? Why wouldn't you want the freedom that comes with knowing you are able to open your own brokerage? Get the highest license possible, as soon as possible.

I don't want the additional liability. In Florida, and perhaps in your state, there is a widespread misconception that having a Broker's license puts additional liability on an agent should a complaint or lawsuit be filed. Let me be frank: if you break a law or are found to have breached an ethical or fiduciary duty, you will be found liable regardless of what license you hold. It is ignorant to assume otherwise. For peace of mind, inquire with your state licensing agency or legal hotline. Unless you learn that your state is an exception, get the highest license possible, as soon as possible.

Every Sales Associate that hangs their license with my brokerage is aware that I expect them to obtain their Broker's license. In recognition of their accomplishment, I incorporate their name and Broker Associate title on the front door. I hope in the near future to be able to say we are a true "Broker's Group." Why should I settle for anything less?

Learn Your Market

There is more to learning your market than memorizing the published county housing statistics – much more. In order to keep your finger on the pulse of your market you must:

- **Conduct Inventory**

  Conducting "inventory" entails physically entering properties in your locale. It does *not* mean scrolling through MLS listings.

The strongest agents are always conducting inventory. They consistently visit new homes listed for sale, regardless of whether they have current clients looking for that type of home. Why? So that when engaged in conversations, they will have quick, house-specific responses: "I was just at 123 Main Street. It's exactly what you are looking for. Would you like me to set up a showing for us?" Who wouldn't want to work with that agent? Such conversations allow you to prove how active and knowledgeable you are in your area.

When you are a new agent, visit a minimum of ten properties a week. Over time, adding inventory of three properties each week, in addition to your listing appointments and buyer showings, should be sufficient. However, *never* stop conducting inventory.

- **Become a Local Expert**

Strong agents know their area like the back of their hand. However most new agents make the mistake of believing they know everything about their area when in fact they only know what their area has to offer someone their age, within their circle of friends, and with similar interests.

Agents old and new should make a point to drive through neighborhoods and visit local offerings they have yet to experience. When you drive residential streets, ask yourself:

- o Is there busy traffic?
- o Do the yards look well kept?
- o Do any of the homes have views (golf course, lake, ocean)?
- o Do the homes appear uniform in style?
- o Do the homes appear uniform in age?
- o Do the homes appear equally kept up?
- o Is there a mix of single- and multi-family homes?
- o Is there a mix of residential and commercial properties?

Note the presence of anything that may affect market value or desirability, be it positive or negative. Landfills, congested traffic areas, railroad tracks, and industrial facilities near a home would likely decrease its value. On the other hand close proximity to public transportation, good schools, a beach, golf course, or water views would increase desirability of a property, and therefore, its market price.

Every now and then, stop and take a photo with a long street view to file with your marketing photos. *Never take photos while standing on private property,* as that would be trespassing and your right to the photograph could be questioned. Extending a camera over a fence may also be considered trespassing. For peace of mind, always take photos standing on public land or right-of-ways.

When you visit parks, memorize what they have to offer (playgrounds, restrooms, kayak rentals, etc.). Be certain to photograph the park, especially beautiful areas and unique features, to use later in marketing materials, websites, or blogs.

Try different restaurants. Out-of-town buyers will, at some point, ask their agent to recommend a restaurant. Know the different types of ethnic restaurants in the area. Be ready to name a couple of special occasion (fine dining) restaurants. Kid-friendly restaurants and good breakfast spots are also asked about often. Order an interesting dish and take a photo. Also, photograph the fronts of the more interesting restaurants. Some of the photos might work great on the community page of your website.

Step outside of yourself and think about what buyers with different needs and interests would want to know, and thus ask you about, when moving to your town. Then seek out the answers. The possibilities are endless, but here are a few examples:

- o Dog owners – locations and hours of dog parks, pet stores, leash laws, recommendations for a veterinarian, knowledge of which homeowner or condo associations allow dogs.

- o Families with children – strengths/weaknesses of area schools, playgrounds, tutoring centers, babysitter recommendations, pediatrician recommendations, sports programs, music programs.

- o Boaters – locations of fixed bridges, locations and hours of public boat launches, cost and availability of boat storage, bait shop locations and hours.

Attend county and town meetings. There is no better way to learn who runs your local government, what developments are being planned, what concerns are being addressed, and about the current strength of the economy. Most meetings are open to the public.

Take every opportunity to learn more about your area. In my opinion, you have no right calling yourself a "local real estate expert" until you have a true grasp on what your area has to offer *all* its citizens.

Learn to Negotiate

Negotiating is both a skill and an art. You owe it to your clients to be an effective negotiator. There are many books written on the subject. Classes are likely offered through your local REALTORS® board. Study and become a strong negotiator.

I will share, however, the one powerful act that will always benefit you, and therefore your clients, during negotiations.

SHUT UP!

That's right – stop talking.

It is human nature to think that the party who can outtalk the other party, by overwhelming them with arguments, will win. On the contrary, it's more likely the quieter of the two walks away with what they wanted.

Why? For the most part, silence makes people uncomfortable. If you can create an uncomfortable silence the other party is going to feel compelled to fill it. And fill it they will. The initially aggressive over-talker will start bumbling around looking for anything to make you respond. They will begin speaking rapidly and back track on their earlier requests. You'll know that you are effective when you start hearing, "Well, maybe my client doesn't need X," or, "Well, I can probably get my client to come around."

Another reason being quiet is effective: if you are not talking, you are listening. By listening, you just might hear something that would allow you to problem solve a point of contention for one party or the other, leading to a positive conclusion to negotiations.

WORKING WITH CLIENTS

First and foremost, know which legal brokerage relationship you are working under, and whether it is presumed or required to be established in writing. If, like Florida, your state has different client/brokerage relationships, understand which relationships hold you accountable to which common laws and fiduciary duties, if any.

If you are a REALTOR®, you will also always abide by the associations Code of Ethics and Professional Standards.

WORKING WITH SELLERS

"You List – You Last," is a common industry phrase. In my opinion those four simple words should be every agent's mantra. While I can't find an individual to attribute to the quote, I am confident he or she was a top producer.

Your advertising dollars and prospecting efforts should always revolve around your current listings or be directed at finding sellers to list their homes. Increase the number of listings and your business will grow exponentially. Why? Because sellers (i.e. listings) are the gift that keep on giving.

- A single listing can fill your pipeline with numerous buyers. A listed home results in *buyers and potentially other sellers reaching out to you* through:

    o Inquiries from your online advertisements

    o Yard sign calls

    o Inquiries from your print advertisements

    o Visiting open houses

    More often than not, buyers that directly contact listing agents are unrepresented. If you are quick to return their communications and able to prove yourself knowledgeable about your listing *and* your local market, it is very likely that these prospective buyers will choose to be represented by you for the purchase or rental of your listed home or another property.

• A single listing can provide a wealth of marketing opportunities. Your name on the yard sign and your contact info and photo attached to the home advertisements both online and in print will get noticed. The more your presence is felt in the community, the better. It signals to residents that you are an active and producing agent. If your name is "familiar" or recognizable to people, you will be at an advantage when competing for future business.

• A single listing allows you to find buyers for the home and receive both sides of the commission, if legal in your state. It is imperative that the agent is conscientious about meeting all ethical, legal, and possibly fiduciary obligations when representing both sides. One will often hear agents label this scenario as "double-dipping." Such a negative connotation speaks to the stigma this practice has. Tread carefully.

Your Obligations to Sellers

First and foremost, understand your listing agreement is a service contract between you, the representative for your brokerage, and the sellers. By accepting a listing, you are acknowledging that you will work to get the home sold and have certain legal obligations to fulfill. For example, the Florida REALTORS® Exclusive Right of Sale Listing Agreement states, "Broker agrees to make diligent and continued efforts to sell the Property until a sales contract is pending on the Property." That is a clearly defined duty – market until pending. However there are other duties and obligations that, while possibly not spelled out in your listing agreement, are understood in the real estate industry as necessary to properly represent one's clients.

Professionals do not "list and pray." Professional listing agents work damn hard to find the right buyers, get their clients the highest price possible, and make the transaction as smooth as possible. If you are unwilling to fulfill the following duties and obligations, you do not deserve the listing.

Have Difficult Discussions Early

If sellers need to be told something, tell it sooner than later. Shying away from necessary discussions helps no one. The sellers hired you to sell their home. If there is something that you believe might impede the sale, you are obligated to bring it to their attention. The earlier you have the discussion, the better received it will be. Have it early and deliver your message succinctly. Constantly revisiting an issue in a wishy-washy manner is unprofessional and an enormous waste of time for both you and your sellers.

- **Pricing**

Perhaps the greatest feared topic of discussion for agents is pricing. The sellers are hiring you to get the highest price possible for the property. Therefore, it is your obligation to educate the sellers as to how impactful pricing the property correctly is.

You must explain that too high of a list price, contrary to what most sellers believe, by and large results in the homeowners making less money on the sale. Overpriced listings linger on market, racking up carrying costs and depleting the sellers' negotiating power each month it sits on market. Stale listings, like stale bread, are not desirable to shoppers. A property listed at or near market price is likely to bring buyers within the area's average time on market. A property listed below market price is likely to get multiple offers quickly, the competition of which can, on occasion, push the final negotiated price to, or above, market price.

Getting sellers to agree on a suggested original list price or a subsequent price reduction causes unnecessary anxiety for agents both new and experienced. There is no reason for any agent to fear such discussions if they have arrived at their pricing strategy based on solid research. The comparative market analysis (CMA), assuming the agent took the time to be thorough and accurate, should do the talking. Agents ought to take a CMA class to learn how to select comparable properties and make appropriate adjustments, so they feel confident about the CMAs they present. An agent must never blindly rely on the comparables and calculations a computer generated CMA program produces. Remember, it is not the agent that is trying to put a price on the property, rather it is the local market that is dictating the price the property will fetch. In fact, an agent never has to state what *they* would price the property at, rather, they should phrase statements so as to remove themselves from the recommendation entirely:

"The local market appears to indicates an appropriate list price of $_____."

"The numbers seem to point to listing your property at $_____."

"Recent sales are suggestive of a $_____list price."

Based on the earlier conversation as to the pros and cons of listing above, below, or at market price, ask the sellers which pricing strategy they would like to employ.

By keeping the suggested price tied to the market and empowering the sellers by allowing them to choose the pricing strategy, the agent should experience little, if any, seller frustration or the dreaded "shoot the messenger" scenario.

Contrary to how most agents work, the best time to discuss when a price reduction would be necessary for a property is *immediately* after establishing the list price, should it be at or above market price. The first price reduction amount and date should be agreed upon and incorporated into the listing agreement during your listing appointment (if allowed by your state). Having planned reductions in writing upfront removes the probability of having to have a reduction discussion when sellers might be in a more emotional state. Discuss why and when price reductions are necessary and why a reduction plan should be set in play. Write it out as such on the listing agreement. However, when working with sellers, refer to a price reduction as a price "modification" or "adjustment." Avoid using the words, or variations of, "reduction, change, lower, drop," which tend to trigger resistance in sellers. "Broker and Sellers agree that on (date) if less than (number) showings have occurred or no offers have been received, the list price will be modified to $XXX,XXX.". If you expect a long time on the market and fear multiple price reductions will be necessary, get a schedule of reductions. "Broker and Sellers agree until an offer is received, the following schedule of price modifications will be in affect: <u>(date then price, date then price, and so on....)</u>" Setting out exact dates and amounts allows you to stagger them so buyers' agents are unable to easily discern a pattern (and thus wait out the next reduction before offering).

Obstinate sellers who insists on outrageously overpricing their homes and refuse to discuss future price reductions may not be worth taking on. By refusing to price within reason, they are displaying they do not respect your expertise and that they are more inclined to work from an emotional rather than a rational state of mind. These sellers are the headaches (not clients) that I warned you about earlier. Taking on exceedingly overpriced listings obligates you to spend time and money with little likelihood of ever getting paid. Moreover, difficult headaches, which overpriced sellers have already proven to be, might prove more litigious in nature than other clients.

• Cleaning

It's not polite to tell someone their home is dirty, so of course agents dread having this conversation. However, you are obligated to help your sellers achieve the highest price for their home, and an unkempt home is certain to derail your efforts. When telling your sellers to clean, choose your words with care. Try to sound positive rather than disgusted or annoyed. "Buyers pay for sparkle! Let's make certain your kitchen and baths shine so we can get top dollar!"

Some sellers may be physically incapable or too limited on time to clean. Offer recommendations of licensed, bonded, and insured cleaning services you trust. A simple, "It's important homeowners clean like crazy before showings. If you would rather have a professional do it, I have several services that my past clients have been very happy with that I could recommend."

Early on, I kept a cleaning caddy in my car so I could tackle anything too horrible before showings. By doing this, I avoided having to have an uncomfortable conversation, but I also devalued my time by becoming a cleaning lady instead of an agent. Your time is of greater value to your sellers when marketing their home than cleaning it.

If the home needs decluttering, say it! Explain that personal photos, mementos, and knickknacks distract potential buyers from viewing the key features of the house, and further, they make it difficult for them to imagine themselves living in it. Having sellers box up such items not only removes clutter, but it also starts the process of emotional detachment from the home, which should result in the sellers being more accepting of offers when they come in. A fun idea is to suggest your sellers hold a garage sale on the same day you are holding an open house to attract additional traffic. Make it a team effort to get the house decluttered and sold!

Create a Unique Marketing Plan for Each Property

Sellers deserve to have a listing agent that is willing to take the time and burden the expense to tailor their marketing efforts to the uniqueness of the home. Marketing should never be one size fits all, nor something an agent just checks off their to-do list. Put time and thought into crafting a unique and strategic marketing plan to best promote the sellers' property. Marketing plans should evolve from the answers to the following questions:

- Which local agents are most likely to have buyers for this property? How should those agents be approached?

- Would this home present better in still photos or video, or both?

- Would this property's location work well for open houses and/or broker tours?

- Do you expect the buyers to come from out of area? If so, what physical areas should you be marketing it in, and with what media (internet, t.v., print, social media, etc.)?

Educate Owners about Disclosures

Every agent must learn the rules regarding disclosures both on the Federal and State levels. For example the Federal Lead-Based Paint Hazard Reduction Act of 1992 requires owners of a residential dwelling unit built prior to 1978 to disclosure any knowledge of lead-based paint or lead-based paint hazards on their property whether sold or rented. As such, all agents must be well-versed regarding lead-based disclosure. Some disclosures are state specific. One such example is whether or not a disclosure must be made if there has been a death in a home, and if so, within the last how many years.

Learn what must be disclosed to prospective buyers and tenants, on which forms the disclosures should be made, if additional information must be provided, such as a supporting brochure, and when the disclosures must take place.

Educate your clients as to the above, and when in doubt, assure them it is better to disclose than not. *Never* state or imply to clients that they should hide a defect or fail to acknowledge a required item of disclosure. Failure-to-Disclose lawsuits against both owners *and real estate agents* are all too common. As such, it is imperative to get all communications about, and the disclosures themselves, in writing. The last thing you need is owners telling a judge that you said an item was not important enough to disclose.

Your state association of REALTORS® will likely have a state customized property disclosure form for use with your sellers. Make certain sellers complete it in their own hand, and have the buyers sign as proof of receipt. Protect your clients. Protect yourself.

Input Complete and Accurate Information into the Multiple Listing Service (MLS)

You owe it to your sellers and landlords to make certain their property is searchable in every possible way and presented in its best light. Moreover, you must make certain the MLS listing is input in such a way as to not expose your clients, yourself, and/or your brokerage to potential liability.

- **Double Check All Information at Its Original Source**

  Most of what you need can be found online or with a simple phone call. Remember, homeowner supplied information, although they may believe it to be true, is often inaccurate.

The local tax appraiser office is an excellent source for par-cel/property identification numbers, lot square footage, munic-ipal assessments, prior year taxes, etc.

The local clerk of courts can provide you with property deeds to double check the owners' names.

Community homeowner and condominium owner associations can provide you with monthly fees, restrictions, pending as-sessments, and more.

- **Revisit your Listing Agreement**

Double check that your offered commissions match your List-ing Agreement terms. Verify that all the items identified to convey in the agreement appear on the MLS. Make certain that if owners wished for an item to be excluded from the sale that you write a phrase such as, "Dining room chandelier does not convey," in the MLS remarks section.

- **Complete Each and Every Input Field**

One never knows what a property's future buyers' search criteria will be. I once had an investor that only wanted to purchase units that could be rented at least four times per year. The number of MLS listings that failed to include minimum rentals per year was staggering. I can only imagine how many suitable properties go unseen every day due to missing searchable criteria on listings.

- **Choose Words Wisely in Your Description**

Discuss the property, *not* the future occupants, in order to avoid discrimination scenarios. Refer to the Fair Housing Act advertising guide applicable for your state. By referencing the Florida guide one would ascertain:

"Walk to town" implies an act of an able-bodied *future occupant* (discriminatory).

"Close proximity to town" describes the Property's relation-ship to the town (safe).

"Perfect starter home for two love birds" implies no children/familial status (discriminatory).

"Small home with lots of charm" implies the size of the home (safe).

If you are uncertain as to material specifics, but want to highlight, for example, that the counters *appear* to be marble, simply state "upgraded counters" for fear that it's a lower quality material than marble. If incorrectly stated on the MLS as marble, should buyers learn differently, they may look to either you or your sellers to physically or financially remedy the discrepancy.

- **Write a Lengthy, Honest, Informative Description**

  The property description will appear on your MLS as well as all websites it syndicates to. People read descriptions.

  Simply writing, "Three bedroom, two bath house with one car garage," is not a captivating description. Your clients deserve more. If you are not good with words, ask a co-worker to help you.

  You are obligated to market the property, and your description is a marketing tool you must give attention to. Use words to help the reader envision living in the home; sell the lifestyle – not just the building.

  Take your time, check your spelling, and use compelling words. If the property is lackluster, discuss the neighborhood or the benefits of homeownership. Let the reader find something of interest in your words.

- **Protect Your Clients, Yourself, and Your Brokerage with Disclaimers**

  While some disclaimers should be used on every listing, others are property specific. Examples include:

"All room dimensions are approximate and not guaranteed; selling agents and buyers should verify."

"Hardship package will be completed and the short sale will be negotiated by seasoned attorney. Final terms and conditions to be approved by a third party, final commission to be split 50/50."

"Shed (or addition, etc.) believed to be unpermitted structure."

"Not ok to advertise or contact owners."

"Dining room drapes (or chandelier, etc.) are excluded from the sale and do not convey."

"Please note the tax rolls list the property as a four bedroom incorrectly; it is a three bedroom property." (Or whatever the difference is in regarding the amount of bedrooms, the lot size, etc.)

"Property not expected to be approved for FHA financing due to XXX (property conditions, appraisal, price, timeframe, etc.)" – Should you not select FHA financing as an option, but do select conventional, this disclaimer keeps its omission from being construed as discriminatory.

- **Include Effective Photos**

  1. Always use your original or personally purchased photos.

     You may not take old listing photos of other agents and upload to your new listing. This would be, at a minimum, a copyright infringement, unless you have express authorization from the agent and possibly their broker. Needless to say, I would get all authorizations in writing and keep this documentation within your property file. Copyright, a federal law, is automatically applied to photographs the minute they are taken, with no need for the photographer to register or submit paperwork of any kind, unlike a trademark or patent.

2. Study your MLS guidelines regarding photos and videos.

    Your local MLS will have rules that dictate inputting of videos and photos. For example, our MLS requires the primary photo must be an exterior front shot of the Property and does not allow branding (any writing on or signage within the photo or video advertising you/your brokerage). Follow your local MLS guidelines.

3. Interior shots require you take your time.

    If possible, try to be alone in the home when taking photos. That way you can feel free to move distracting items to the floor or around the corner and out of the shot, stand on a chair to take a down angle, and take your time in each room all without upsetting the homeowners. At minimum, always shut toilet lids, remove garbage cans, pet food bowls, dirty clothes, etc. from the shot. If certain items are not to convey with the home, attempt to keep them out of the shots. When removing a large number of items from the room, take a "before" picture so you can refer back to where all the items should go. Take the same photo with and without a flash. Photograph each room from various locations, angles, and heights. Leaving a property with 100+ shots that you can select from, as opposed to only one from each room, is strongly suggested for the best results.

4. The exterior shot is your money shot.

    Every piece of marketing will be centered on it. Give it the attention it deserves. A property's exterior shot requires a bit of creativity. Your job is to increase or create virtual curb appeal. A straight-on shot of a home from the street, while the most common, can be the least likely to engage prospective buyers. Try angling the shot to capture the corner of the home, allowing for depth. Frame a shot to highlight a winding walkway, charming porch, or impressive front door. Shoot at dusk with all interior and exterior lights on for a dramatic feel. Have an aerial shot taken for larger properties. Remember to have all cars removed from the driveway (unless you are strategically staging the shot with a luxury vehicle).

5.   Select, edit and organize photos thoughtfully.

Hopefully you have over 100 photos to sort through. Once uploaded to your computer, do a quick run through and delete those which editing cannot correct (horrible angles, pitch dark, etc.). Do not keep a photo simply because it is the only one of a room — *it is better for a room not to appear in photos than to be shown poorly*. Unless it is a key selling point to a particular property, do not include photos of closets, half-baths, attics, garage interiors, and similar unattractive, utilitarian spaces.

Photos that remain should be edited. Crop, level, adjust brightness, and do whatever is necessary to make the pictures the best they can be. Once edited, organize the pictures in one of two ways, either to capture the flow of the home, or to highlight its best rooms first. Which organization you use is highly dependent on the individual home. If you are marketing the "lifestyle" the home would bring to its new owners, order the pictures according to how one would walk through the home. If the home has upgraded kitchens and baths, unlike the neighbor's similar properties, place the kitchen and baths first to increase the likelihood that they are viewed.

6.   Add community photos after the home photos.

If the home is in an association with amenities (pool, tennis courts, riding trails), make certain to include photos of each. If the home is in close proximity to sporting venues, downtown shops and dining, nature preserves, the beach, etc., make sure to include photos of these desirable selling points as well.

7. Label your photos.

This step is ignored by too many agents. Help the prospective buyers understand what they are viewing while taking the opportunity to highlight features as well. Bathrooms are an excellent example of why labeling is so important; it is extremely difficult to visually distinguish between baths. Labeling a photo "Guest Bath" helps the viewer mentally attach it to the guest bedroom. Labeling it "Guest Bath w/Heated Floors" also allows for you to include a non-visual selling point.

8. Videos increase viewership.

Most photographers now include videos in their packages. Always include video if the property is staged or professionally decorated. For other listings, a simple video option is to create a montage of your best edited photos set to music, which will increase traffic on the listing.

• **Keep Information Up to Date**

The MLS listing should always be revisited and checked for needed changes. Perhaps you had indicated initially that a tenant's lease was to expire in January, but in fact, they have now extended to stay until June – correct the month of lease termination. Have showing instructions changed? Did homeowner association fees increase since you created the listing? It is your job to keep your MLS listings as timely as possible.

Secure Your Clients' Property

Your clients trust you to keep their property safe. Ideally, you will be present at all showings. However, you should always plan for the alternative. There is no reason to use code lockboxes today. Spend the money required for the electronic lockboxes that work with your MLS. Program the boxes to:

• Block access after 9 p.m. and before 8 a.m.;

- Notify you immediately when a key is accessed and send you the showing agent's contact info;

- Prompt the agent with reminders, i.e. "Please check that all sliders are locked before leaving;"

- Send feedback requests to all who showed.

Upon taking a listing of an unoccupied home, visit the surrounding neighbors, introduce yourself, and provide your business card. Explain that you are selling the home and that showings will take place and you would greatly appreciate if they would call you if anything ever appears amiss. What could be better? You get extra sets of eyes on the home *and* leave an impression on potential sellers that not only are you active in the area, but you also care deeply about the clients and homes you represent.

And of course, always pop into your unoccupied properties in the evening to check if they were properly secured after any unaccompanied showings.

Troubleshoot Potential Closing Issues Before You Have Buyers

A professional listing agent will always thoroughly research the property and try to uncover potential contractual holdups and pitfalls as soon as they take the listing. Early troubleshooting allows agents to stay ahead of their deals, rather than chasing behind them.

Research if there are open permits, and if so, work with the owners to close them. No need to have buyers walk from a contract over an open permit that could have been corrected prior.

If applicable, learn the governing association's approval process. What would result in a denial? How long is approval expected to take? Do not waste anyone's time accepting a contract from someone who will not be approved. Moreover, don't accept or draft any contracts that fail to allow appropriate time for the approval to be granted.

Research what mortgage product will work for the home. Condo associations often fail to meet the criteria banks need to lend. If the property is within a condo association, provide your mortgage broker the address to learn what type of financing is possible. You do not want to remove the property from the market for buyers with the wrong type of financing.

Obtain an insurance quote for the property. If you learn the property is uninsurable or subject to extremely high insurance rates due to the age of roof, flood zone, etc., you will need to problem solve with your sellers. Alert your sellers to the possible insurance dilemma you expect buyers to encounter. Time is money – and you do not want your sellers to accept a contract from buyers who will not be able to close on the property. For example, if the age/condition of the roof is the issue, you could suggest that the sellers:

- Invest in a new roof being put on *now*, and off-set the cost with a higher list price, likely re-opening the home to buyers with conventional, FHA, and VA financing.

- Only accept cash buyers (as lenders will not finance if the home cannot be insured.)

Title issues are also best cleared up before a contract is accepted. If there is any question as to who should be signing for the home sale (death of a party on the deed, homeowner with dementia, missing persons from a deed), put the situation in front of a title officer. You might need time to resolve the issue by obtaining an original death certificate, acquiring physician letters to invoke a power of attorney, or tracking down out-of-area owners.

Present All Offers in Their Best Light

Just because an offer comes in low, do not assume that those who submitted are not your buyers. Present low offers to your sellers with enthusiasm. Explain that it is better to have an offer you can negotiate than not have an offer at all. If you act positive about the fact that you finally have something to work with, your sellers are less likely to be offended. You do not want angry sellers that shut down communication before you have the opportunity to get the buyers up to their highest and best offer.

Guide your sellers through the entire offer. Never let them stop at the price. If favorable terms are within, highlight those as items you won't have to negotiate for.

Explain to your sellers that there are many people who feel compelled to throw a low number first, so they can sleep at night knowing they tried to get a steal. After the first counter, they often relax and negotiate reasonably from there on out.

Ask your sellers to counter with a small price reduction to indicate they refuse to settle anywhere near the offer, yet are willing to negotiate. Assure your sellers that if the buyers don't come around, they are not your buyers, no harm no foul. However, if they do come up to an acceptable price, after a couple counters, the sellers will be glad they rolled the dice.

Control the Contract Drafting

Yes, the buyers' agent submitted the contract, and yes, the other agent might be more experienced then you. However, do not let yourself become intimidated by the other side. If it is not as clean as you believe it should be due to blanks not being filled in, ambiguous wording, dates that don't line up, etc., explain to your sellers why you would like to alter specific items (assuming you legally can in your state), and get the changes sent back with the counter. Have your sellers initial next to the alterations, and make certain the other side does as well. If the necessary changes are extensive, simply draft a new contract for your sellers to sign and then present to the other side for signatures.

If something on the contract is confusing to you, call the other agent to discuss. I have yet to meet a buyers' agent that isn't happy for the chance to discuss an offer with a listing agent.

Monitor all Contract Dates

The minute you are under contract, put all important dates into your phone and list on a sheet in the file. When are the deposits due? When are the loan and association applications to be made by? When does the Inspection Period end? When is loan approval to be completed? When is title to be provided by? When is closing to occur? You must be on top of dates and timeframes in that contract. When they tick close, communicate with the buyers' agent and make sure the deadlines will be met. Obtain written confirmation of deposits, approvals, etc. If you want to protect your deal from falling apart, it is in your best interest to make sure the other side does not fail to perform in a timely manner.

Physically be Present

You agreed to represent your sellers in the sale of their property. I believe the only way to do that is by being physically present, in their stead, at all showings, inspections, appraisals, and the closing.

- **Showings**

    Why be present at showings? That's what lockboxes are for. Their buyers' agent is with them…

    Who better to overcome buyers' objections than the listing agent? You know the property. Give the tour. Highlight features. Answer questions. Why should your sellers expect anything less?

    However, NEVER overstep your boundaries with the other agent by trying to become personal with their buyers. Simply show the home and then give them private time to revisit any rooms of interest and speak among themselves. If the buyers have questions you do not have the immediate answer to, assure them you will research the answer and get it over to their agent as soon as possible.

    Another reason to attend showings is to get immediate feedback to share with your sellers. If you rely on the buyers' agent to provide feedback, you may never get any, or perhaps be fed a generic response. If you are in the home with the buyers, you will be able to gauge how much they emotionally connected with the home. Did they take their time in the kitchen, open cabinets, and make a positive remark on the appliance brands? Did they talk with their agent about whether or not their furniture would fit the space? Did they scoff at the materials used? Did they say they didn't care to see the garage? Being present at showings gives you valuable insight to share with your sellers as to how truly motivated the buyers behind any offer likely are.

- **Home Inspections**

When working as a listing agent, I always try to be present during home inspections. Once again, the listing agent knows the home and is often the only one present that can possibly help problem solve a finding to which an inspector would have no knowledge of its origin or history. Do note, it is the listing agent's duty to make certain all utilities are on at the property so the inspection can be properly conducted. Should you be representing a vacant home, alert the owners to this fact a few days prior to the scheduled inspection so they have time to get them turned on, if need be. Strongly suggest your sellers NOT be present during the inspection. Sellers are quick to become emotional when their home is "picked apart." Assure your sellers that you will be present through the duration of the inspection and will call them for clarification should the inspector have any questions.

At the start of the inspection, introduce yourself to the inspector and let he or she know that you will be present in the home until completion. State that you are happy to get the homeowners on the phone if any questions arise. Then spend the next few hours getting some work done on your phone or laptop while the buyers and their agent interact with their inspector.

Do not overstep your boundaries; this is the buyer's due diligence, not yours. Take notes and photos if the inspector calls you over to point something out. Listen carefully and ask the inspector to explain further anything you do not understand. Never be argumentative. These interactions with the inspector provide you, and thus your sellers, a better understanding of problems in the home. Some inspectors give a verbal summary of their findings to everyone present (including the listing agent), others may not. Listen if you are included, but keep in mind, many of the issues may have little, if any, bearing on the transaction. The only inspection issues that are of concern are those the buyer formally requests in writing for the seller to repair.

A word of caution, do NOT have the sellers repair *any* items brought up by the inspector prior to a formal written request from the buyers. Sellers believe they are fixing a problem when in fact they might be creating a new problem. For example, if your sellers had their friend repair an item, but the buyers make a formal request a day later stating they will only accept a licensed and bonded professional to make the repair, you now have a situation on your hands.

- **Appraisals**

  The listing agent's presence at an appraisal is essential. Provide the appraiser with everything you are legally allowed to make his or her job easier. Arrive with MLS listings of comparables (comps) that support the list price. The foundational criteria appraisers look for in comps are:

  1. within the same subdivision, or else within one half mile of the subject property without crossing hard lines (expressways or waterways);

  2. within 20% of square footage under air;

  3. **sold** within the last six months

  If an agent has personal knowledge of any homes that might meet the above criteria yet should not be allowed as comps for a listing due to, for instance, extensive mold or problematic deferred maintenance issues that were neither photographed nor noted in the description on the MLS, provide those printouts with notes to their condition as well. In Florida, an agent may provide their card stapled to the front of the contract and a list of recent upgrades to the home compiled by the homeowners (and noted as such) with corresponding receipts.

Simply hoping the appraisal comes in at the contract price is not representing your sellers. It sets your sellers up to possibly have to reduce the contract price to keep the buyers' financing in play or emotions in check. You owe it to your sellers to do everything in your power to help the property appraise at the highest price possible.

- **Closings**

    Prior to the closing, confirm that your sellers' have the time, date, and location correct. Make certain the spouse (if any) will attend and that both bring their state issued driver's licenses.

    You should bring with you the full paper transaction file and keys to the property.

    Always attend closings. No, not just to pick up the commission check. Attend so you are there for your sellers when something goes wrong. Do things always go wrong? No. But you were hired to see your sellers through the home sale, and until it funds, you are not done representing them. Be there until the end. Be a calming presence and keep your clients' emotions in line if it becomes rocky.

    Be a problem solver. The buyers found a hole in the wall from the sellers' movers an hour before closing? Get everyone in the "things happen" state of mind. Confirm with the sellers that matching paint is still present in the home. Get a handyman you know on speaker to provide a general estimate and have your sellers credit the buyers the amount of estimate and schedule the handyman to meet the new buyers at the home that afternoon to make repair. The wife forgot her driver's license at her office? Offer to run to her work and pick it up from a co-worker. Whatever comes at you — be the problem solver and keep everyone calm and moving forward.

Keep in Constant Communication with Your Sellers

At minimum, reach out to your sellers as agreed upon in your Client/Agent Communications Expectations form. However, even if they told you only to contact them when you have something to report, I believe you should never let a week go by without checking in. Selling one's home is a stressful time; days seem to tick away at a snail's pace. In the beginning, every morning the homeowners are hoping that it will be the day you call to say you have an offer. Each night they are disappointed an offer never arrived. During the contract phase, they worry if the buyers are performing their duties, if the home inspection will be problematic, if the appraisal has come in, if closing will happen on time, and many other details. It's a very emotional experience, and they should never feel abandoned by the person they trusted to get them through it. From the day you take the listing until the day after closing, make a point to call, email, and/or text your sellers – often.

WORKING WITH BUYERS

Many agents favor working with buyers as it can be very emotionally rewarding. It is more common for agents to form deep relationships with buyers than sellers. Buyers usually enjoy showings; they are excited to find their new home. Buyers and agents spend hours together driving and touring properties, allowing the opportunity for a friendship to grow. At the end, the agents get to hand their new friends the key to their dream homes and the start of their new lives...can it get better than that?

Unfortunately, as working with buyers can be such a personal experience and emotional high for agents, it can prove hard for agents to control their financial stake in the transaction and keep their professional duties front and center.

Your Obligations to Buyers

You owe your buyers strength and competency, not friendship. They hired a professional to find them a home in their criteria that they can afford. They already have friends; they need a real estate agent.

Qualify Buyers – Always

Have you heard the industry phrase, "Buyers are Liars?" It's an expression agents use to justify when their buyers continually change search criteria, defect to other agents, or decide not to buy altogether. Please understand when buyers do any of the previous it is more likely the result of agents failing to properly qualify, provide value, or establish a professional working relationship than a conspiracy of compulsive liars out to get our industry.

Always set a time to meet with potential buyers *before* showing properties. Explain it is important that you get 20 minutes of their time so you can tailor your service to their needs. Your meeting will allow you to understand desired criteria for their future home, their finances, and their time frame. With this meeting and information, you can be as effective as possible for them.

Do not be swayed by the person that tries to push you off, "they want to see a few homes first" or "he'll know the right house when he sees it – just set up some showings." That person will never be a client. At best, they are a headache, and you should immediately, politely, and firmly direct them to seek out another agent to help them with their home search. Remember, working with buyers that do not purchase ALWAYS COSTS YOU MONEY WITH NO POSSIBLE RETURN ON INVESTMENT, unlike a failed listing where one could argue it still provided advertising opportunities to acquire other leads. Allowing time to service uncommitted buyers is probably the poorest business decision an agent could make.

Conduct the qualifying meeting as follows:

- **Meet either in your office or at a public location.**

  An office conference room or local coffee shop works great. You need a table or desk to pass papers across, and these locations provide a safe setting to meet strangers for the first time.

- **Always dress professionally.**

  Even if you have met with the buyers in a non-real estate related setting prior, dress professionally as it sets the tone for the seriousness of the business transaction you are working towards.

- **Learn their criteria.**

  After introductions, your conversation should start by working through their needs vs. wants in a home. Their dislikes (hates/nevers) should also be discussed. Dig deep to find what would immediately turn them off as it might not be a typical search criteria item that would come up during the course of general conversation. For example, I HATE bay windows in the front of a home. I would never, ever, ever consider buying a home with a bay window on the front exterior. I had a client that would NEVER live in a unit that was near the building's trash chute. Neither of these features would appear on any agent's checklist of criteria to discuss with their buyers. There is nothing more frustrating than having spent time researching and then showing a property to only learn they were never going to consider it as a result of a visceral dislike for one feature.

  I like to draw two lines down a piece of paper to create three columns. The left column is labeled "Needs", the center, "Wants," and the right, "Never." This sheet serves multiple purposes. First, it lets the clients know that I am listening to them and have every intention to find them what they want. Second, the sheet is a quick reference for me when creating the automated search on the MLS. Third, I have a copy of it on hand during all showings to reference with them should they start to become overwhelmed or indecisive.

- **Ask about their finances**.

  Now that they know you are a careful note taker and committed to their search, it is time to ask about how they plan to purchase the home, with cash or financing?

If they are cash buyers, explain the local customs in your area as to the amount of deposit that is likely necessary and when first and second deposits are typically due (so they can make certain those monies are in an account that can be quickly liquidated). Also alert them to the fact that, to submit an offer, the sellers are going to require proof of funds for the entire sale amount for it to be considered. Proof of funds might be financial statements with social security and account numbers blacked out except for the four last digits, or else a signed letter on a financial institution's letterhead stating the buyers have $XXX,XXX amount in funds deposited, or other such documentation. If the funds are not in typical checking or savings accounts, ask the buyer to call the financial holder and learn in what time frame the funds can be moved. If there is a long wait time, you will have to determine the closing date accordingly.

If the buyers plan to use financing, ask if they have met with a mortgage broker recently. If not, provide them with two copies of your List of Preferred Related Industry Professionals. It should include three mortgage brokers, three home inspectors, three real estate attorneys/title companies, and three insurance brokers. Why three? Because this limits your liability from being accused of having steered them towards a single resource that they might have a problem with. They should keep one copy and *sign and date the other* for you to include in your records. Explain that a mortgage broker will hold their hand through the process and that the hardest part is getting together the financial information the loan officer needs to review. Get them in the mindset that the best use of their immediate time is to get pre-approved as soon as possible if they truly wish to buy in the near future.

If they state they already have met with a mortgage broker, ask if they were provided a pre-qualification or pre-approval letter. Ideally they would have brought it with them, but if not, ask for the mortgage broker's information and their permission to reach out to him or her. Keep in mind, being pre-qualified in most instances means that their financial records were not reviewed, and thus pre-qualification holds little weight. Read the pre-qualification to try to ascertain if the financials have in fact been reviewed or call the loan officer on the letter and ask what the qualification entailed. The pre-approval letter is usually what you are striving for.

Do not forget to ask where the money for the down payment and monies brought to the table are coming from. If it is a family gift or cash they have been hiding in their mattress, stress they discuss the situation with the mortgage broker so all money is properly documented (a letter from the gifting party), sourced (its origins found), and seasoned (been in the buyers' account long enough) if need be, to avoid a delay of closing.

- **Ask about their current living situation.**

If they need to sell a home before purchasing the next, that scenario likely outed itself during the cash vs. financing conversation. Should that be the case, do not let them convince you to show them homes until at minimum their existing home is on the market, but more ideally, wait until once their home is under contract. Explain that it is unlikely that any sellers would agree to tie up their property by accepting an offer contingent on the sale of a home that is not already under contract. You would never suggest they stop marketing and showing their existing home for buyers that have yet to bother listing their property; why would any other agent? Also point out that by asking sellers for such a contingency, they have greatly diminished their ability to negotiate other terms such as price or repairs. Should they understand and accept your advice, set an appointment to view their existing home as soon as possible so you can get it listed. Complete the meeting with the understanding that your remaining discussion is more for them to learn how the buying process works than to get started on viewing homes, as that will have to wait until their existing home is on the market.

Renters might need to close on a home by their lease end. If their lease will be ending sooner than you expect to be able to close on a home, ask them to speak with their landlords about possibly going month to month. Should the landlords be unwilling, you will have to get them prepared for a quick home search and problem solve with them for temporary living solutions. Buyers in leases with end dates months away should be asked to review their lease to determine if there is a termination offer or break lease clause within. Such a clause would allow them to pay to be released early. If so, the cost of the release should be factored in to their decision to bid on any home they find prior to lease end. Another option is to review the lease for the right to sublet. However, while subletting might provide them with the money to cover the rent until lease end, do alert them to the fact that subletting does not remove them from liability should their substitute tenants fail to pay, cause damage to the unit, etc. If the lease end date and terms are too problematic, your only course of action might be to direct them to wait for a few months before starting their home search.

- **Discuss the price range they wish to view homes in.**

Your market expertise is crucial in such discussions. All too often buyers want to view homes above what they can afford. A professional agent will not show homes outside the buyers' price range. If they have yet to get pre-approved, they might not know their price range yet. Regardless, explain why viewing homes above budget with the intention to low ball wastes everyone's time and sets them up for disappointment...not a great bargain. If you know that homes are averaging 93% of list price, share that statistic with the buyers to counter their intention to offer 60 cents on the dollar. Never attend a qualification appointment without statistics at the ready to counter unreasonable negotiation expectations. Do not let buyers leave your meeting believing that you will spend your valuable time writing and submitting offers on their behalf that have no chance of being accepted. If that is what the buyers are looking for in an agent, they are headaches, and you need to direct them to find another agent to work with.

- **Keep your ears open for any trouble indicators.**

During the meeting, be on the lookout for any red flags the buyers may wave. When discussing the area in which they wish to live, or not live, were any comments or jokes of a discriminatory nature made? Did the buyers mention they have already viewed 50 homes, or burned through multiple agents? Do the buyers try to interrupt you or correct you when you speak? The list of warning signs that buyers are a liability or headaches rather than future clients is long and varied. Always listen to your gut, and do not work with any buyers that make you uncomfortable in any way. One home sale is NOT worth losing your license over.

- **Explain your value to the transaction.**

Once you have vetted the buyers and wish to accept them as clients, explain how you will help them achieve their goals. That success will be the result of a strong partnership and you are honored that they chose you to work alongside them.

Outline the order of events that need to occur for you to be able to help them find their new home. Perhaps they have to be pre-approved before you can know their true price point; perhaps their existing home has to be listed before you can start looking for their next.

Explain the typical chronology of a home purchase – sorting through listings, showings, offer, deposits, inspections, financing approval, appraisal, survey, title work, closing. Answer any questions they may have and assure them you will hold their hand through the entire process.

Assure them that you can help them with new construction, resale, and homes advertised as For Sale By Owner (FSBOs). Explain the nuances of working with each and why it is essential for them to have buyer representation through the transaction. Thus they must always allow *you to make first contact* with all construction communities, listing agents, and FSBO's.

- **Get preliminary paperwork signed.**

  Signing paperwork creates a psychological commitment for the buyers to both the home buying process and to you, the agent. It also eliminates the concern that you might forget to provide the forms later, when you are involved in generating an offer. Some examples of forms that could be signed at the qualification meeting:

  - *List of Preferred Related Industry Professionals* (if not signed earlier during the financing discussion)

  - *Buyers' Disclosure* (state or broker form)

  - *Energy Efficiency Brochure* (state form)

  - *Protect Your Family from Lead Based Paint* (HUD brochure)

  - *Affiliated Business Arrangement Disclosure Statement* (HUD form)

  - *Client/Agent Communications Expectations* (Broker or Agent form.)

  I would also provide the buyers with a sample copy of the contract for sale and purchase you expect their offer to be presented on. Ask them to read it at their leisure and to reach out to you with any questions they may have. Too many buyers see the contract for the first time when an agent is asking them to sign an offer, which is a highly emotionally charged moment in time.

- **Obtain an Exclusive Buyer Brokerage Agreement**

  The strongest agents will protect their time and commission with an Exclusive Buyer Brokerage Agreement or similar form that obligates the broker (agent) to perform outlined duties and the buyers to compensate the broker for such performance. In essence, it is an exclusive service contract similar to a Listing Agreement. When the buyers close on a home and the broker (agent) is compensated by a cooperative commission from the sellers' side, the buyers' obligation to pay the broker is waived. If the sellers do not pay your commission (for example a FSBO or unregistered new construction) the buyers will pay. If buyers are serious about using you, he/she will not hesitate to sign such an agreement.

Return a copy of all forms, disclosures, and the Buyer Brokerage Agreement via email or by hand to the buyers within 24 hours of their signing, as is best practice with any paperwork buyers sign.

Respect Your Buyers' Time

An agent shows respect for buyers' time by only showing homes that meet their criteria, researching the homes prior to showings, and by adding value during the showings.

- **Set Buyers Up On an Automated Home Search.**

  Use the criteria identified in the qualifying meeting to set an MLS search to deliver matching properties to buyers every morning (or an interval that they prefer.) Let the buyers know that you will configure the search as accurately as possible; however, it is only as good as the listing agents' input, and therefor on occasion a rogue property may appear. You do not want them calling you needlessly to complain every time a property that does not match their criteria is sent. Instruct buyers to notify you when a property is of interest, at which time you will research it further. If the research does not uncover anything that would disqualify the property, you will set up a showing that works with their and the sellers' schedules.

- **Research the homes prior to showings.**

  Beyond digesting the MLS and any attached documents that might be attached to the listing, at minimum I would know the following about each property:

o   Year and amount the property last sold for;

o   If the property is mortgaged, for how much?

o   If vacant, for how long?

o   If rented, for how much?

o   The current taxes amount and if the current homeowners claim exemptions;

o   If under an association, what are the fees and what do they cover?

o   What the last three homes in the neighborhood sold for.

Ideally, you would have time to create an entire CMA to bring to the showing, and if you are a new agent with the time to do so, I would strongly suggest it. Most busy agents, however, will only prepare CMA's on homes their buyers intend to offer on.

- **Set Up Showings**

Try to limit showings to two or three homes to keep the buyers focused and keep the homes distinct in their minds.

Showings should be scheduled according to the instructions on the MLS, which will direct you to schedule an appointment online, call, or email the listing agent. Always follow the instructions to the letter. Just because there is a lockbox on the door does NOT mean you have the right to enter a property.

The order in which you show is important. Granted, it is often dictated by when sellers allow the showing. However if you can control the order, you will have to decide if you want to show the "best" home first or last.

Showing the best home first may save you time if they immediately fall in love, want to make an offer, and express no interest in seeing others. However, in my experience, if buyers know three homes are lined up, even if they absolutely love the first one, they seem compelled to still view the others.

If you show homes in worst, better, best order, the last home will certainly be appreciated as they will have the earlier homes to draw from for comparisons.

I personally prefer to keep my showings limited to two homes. I schedule *two* appointments for the best home, one before and one after the second home which I do not expect them to like as much. After showing the second home, if my buyers are still reminiscing about the first, I already have an appointment set up to let me bring them back. I look like a hero, and they get the extra time needed to emotionally connect with the home. Of course, if upon leaving the first showing I know that they are not interested, I call the agent to let them know that I will not be returning for the other I set up. If they do not put in an offer on one of the homes, I will find two more for them to view the next day.

- **Conduct Showings**

  At minimum bring copies of the MLS report (private for you, public for the buyers), the tax appraiser report, and either MLS listings of recent comps or a full CMA. The more information you have at the ready the better.

  If the listing agent is accompanying, ask them to show the property. Be respectful by listening to the other agent and following after your clients. When appropriate, ask questions. This should never be an attempt to upstage the other agent, but rather to learn what your research was unable to uncover.

  Always work to show the property in its best light. Park on the street so they can experience the curb appeal and the long walk up the driveway. Turn on all lights and open all window coverings so the home is bright and cheery. Do not rush through the home; let them experience it at their own pace.

As you walk the home, do not point out the superficial details. They don't need a professional to tell them the drapes are lovely. Share what you learned through your research. Discuss the amenities in the community, energy saving features of the home, the benefit of having the particular roofing material the home has, etc.

If you observe something potentially problematic – point it out. Deferred maintenance issues, floors which seem to be sloping, evidence of mold, pests, etc. If you identify problems with the lot, poor drainage, or a neighbor's fence that appears to encroach the property, show your buyers. You are obligated to let them know what your years of experience allow you to see. Regardless of what appears wrong, do not include your emotions into the discussion. What might terrify you, may not phase your buyers, or vice versa. You are not buying the home. Remind them that they will have a home inspector out to gauge the situation and they can use their due diligence period to get quotes from contractors, if need be.

Always ask clients to step outside the home while you take a moment to lock up. Suggest they explore the garden or stroll down the street to see the neighboring homes. You are obligated to make certain the home is secured and in the condition you found it. If you are engaged in conversation with your clients it is too easy to become distracted and leave a light on, a curtain open, or a sliding door unlocked. Take your time, make certain to double check all locks, and leave your business card on the foyer table or kitchen counter should that be your local custom.

Carefully Draft Offers

Always contact the listing agent before drafting an offer. Ask if they are under contract or currently in possession of any offers. Why would you get your buyers' hopes up and waste everyone's time writing an offer on a property that is no longer available? Should the agent inform you that they are currently in possession of another offer, or have been told another offer is coming in, you must alert your buyers that they may want to make a more aggressive offer than originally planned in order to be competitive. Ask if the sellers have any specific terms or conditions that are important to them. For example, the agent might share with you that the sellers do not want to move before a certain date, they would like to hold the note at 6% interest, etc. Share this information with your buyers.

The buyers' agent drafts the original offer, assuming the buyers have not hired an attorney to do so. Therefore, you set the standard for the paperwork. As previously discussed, take your time and fill in all blanks, make certain all numbers add up, time frames work, and all addendums/riders are included. If the addendum/rider should not be signed by buyers until sellers make a disclosure on the form, still include it *without* buyers' signatures as a placeholder to make certain it is not forgotten in the transaction. Double check the buyers initialed and signed in all applicable places.

Help the buyers make their offer as strong as possible. If their offer is low, shore it up with favorable terms, such as shortening the Inspection Period (within reason), a quick close, putting down a larger deposit, etc. Terms are powerful bargaining tools. It is not uncommon for sellers to choose a lower price offer if the terms are more favorable.

Submit Offers in a Professional Manner

Your offer submittal sets the tone for the transaction. Always be thoughtful about how the offer will be received from the other side. The email you send speaks volumes. Whether subconsciously or consciously, listing agents will present an offer to the sellers more positively if they believe the other agent is someone they would like to work with.

- **The Offer Email**

    Write, "Offer – (Property Address)" on the subject line so the other agent will open it.

Start with a salutation of your choice and the other agent's first name properly spelled. Thank them for having allowed you to show their property and state you are now submitting an offer. Identify what attachments you have included (offer, pre-approval letter, proof of funds, comps). If you know your offer to be low and your buyers have given you permission to indicate that they are willing to negotiate, state, "I hope this offer opens communications between the buyers and sellers." Sign off the email with, "Looking forward to working with you."

As discussed earlier, your signature should have your full contact information as well as the two disclaimers regarding the email is to be destroyed if sent to wrong recipient, and, that the email in itself does not create a binding contract.

Double check all spelling, punctuation, and that all attachments are present before sending.

Always use tracking and set the email with a read receipt, for both piece of mind that the other side received it and documentation should the date and time of receipt ever need to be argued.

- **Following Up the Email**

  If you submitted the offer late at night, wait to follow up until the morning. If the submission was within work hours, either call or text the agent to alert them to the fact you sent it over. Should the agent answer the call, be polite and pleasant, state that you just sent over an offer and that you are looking forward to working with them.

Be a Strong Negotiator

As discussed earlier, you owe it to your buyers to effectively negotiate for them.

Keep in mind, especially when representing buyers, being a strong negotiator does not always mean beating up the other side over the sale price.

Being a strong negotiator means getting the other side to agree to, or come as close as possible to, what your buyers want. Sometimes your buyers just want the house, plain and simple. They don't want to risk losing it over a few thousand dollars. Respect whatever offer they wish you to present, even if you think you could get the home for less, do not push. You are not buying the house, they are.

Monitor all Contract Dates

The minute you are under contract, put all important dates into your phone and list on a sheet in the file. It is your job to make certain your clients meet *all* deadlines and that proof of performance is provided to the listing agent. Should you learn that your clients need more time to attend to one item or another, you must get an extension signed by all parties of the contract to protect your clients' deposits. Do not count on the listing agent to remind you of important deadlines.

If there is a date or timeframe in that contract you must stay on top of it.

Be Physically Present

You agreed to represent your buyers in the purchase of their next home. I believe the only way to do that is by being physically present, alongside them or in their stead, at all showings, inspections, appraisals, and the closing.

- **Showings**

  Of course you have to be present at showings! How else could you gauge your clients' reaction to the property, share what you learned through your research, and/or point out any possible problems you observe?

  I have had an agent or two in the past ask if I could show my listing to their clients when they were unavailable. This is not something I recommend.

  Always try to reschedule if a true emergency arises, or send a co-associate from your brokerage in your place. Why? Because unless you know that listing agent very well, or your clients have signed an Exclusive Buyer Brokerage Agreement, you are placing your representation of those buyers in jeopardy. Should that listing agent "poach" your buyers, you will only have yourself to blame. Although procurement rules vary from state to state, solely setting up a showing appointment is unlikely to win a procuring cause dispute if the listing agent did end up representing those buyers throughout a transaction to close.

- **Home Inspections**

No home inspection should ever occur without the buyers' agent present. At the start of the inspection, introduce yourself to the inspector. If your buyers are unable to be present (not recommended – but it happens), let him or her know that you will be present throughout the inspection and would greatly appreciate being called to view anything found of great import and that you are looking forward to listening to the verbal summary at the end of the inspection. Ask in advance that he or she be understanding that, as they are not present, the buyers might reach out via phone or email after receiving the report for additional clarification. Express that you'd greatly appreciate if they would answer any questions the buyers have. Then interact with their inspector only when appropriate. Do not hover over them, but remain readily available. Take notes and photos when you are called for. Listen carefully and ask any questions you may have for the inspector. Try to draw as much out of the inspector as possible regarding any items of concern. Never be argumentative. These interactions with the inspector are invaluable.

Once the report is received (usually sent to the buyers who would then forward to you), carefully comb through it. All buyers have their threshold of acceptable repairs, which is determined by cost, physical labor, or unwillingness to live through repairs – perhaps all three. Listen to your buyers' level of comfort or discomfort with the items in the report. Explain their options, which are often walk away from the property (be certain to determine if their deposit would be at risk and advise accordingly), ask for repairs and/or credit, or accept the property as is. Do not push them into a decision they will later want to rescind, as it might not be possible without great expense.

- **Appraisals**

  If your buyers' financing could be in jeopardy, unless you are certain the property will appraise at or above the purchase price, coordinate with the listing agent to be present (the appraiser will call the listing agent to set the appointment). If the listing agent does not plan to do the prep work to provide all that is allowed to the appraiser, take the task upon yourself as was outlined earlier in the Appraisals bullet point in the Obligations to Sellers' section.

  Your buyers, especially cash buyers with appraisal contingencies, may want you to highlight comps to the appraiser that would argue the price lower than the contract price. Some buyers ask you not to interact with the appraiser at all. Always respect your clients' wishes.

- **Final Walk-Throughs**

  Up to this point, as an agent, you have hopefully done everything within your power to assure the final walk-through should be just that, the *final* walk-through.

  When to schedule a final walk-through is an important decision. You never want to have your buyers accept the property's condition before the tenants or sellers have completely vacated the property. Yet, you don't want to conduct it on your way to closing either. If an issue is identified, you want time to remedy it so the closing will not have to be delayed.

  Call the listing agent a few days before closing to discuss the sellers' moving schedule. Let the other agent know you will not conduct the walk-through until they have vacated. Moreover, remind the agent of any items that are not to convey (the old refrigerator in the garage, the stacks of lumber along the fence, the old boxes in the attic) and are expected to be removed from the property. Also ask the agent to remind the sellers to leave those items that must convey but occupants unknowingly or intentionally take (curtains, washer/dryers, central vacuum attachments, pool cleaners, new refrigerator in garage, etc.). Don't allow yourself to be the agent who gets blindsided by owners who have yet to start packing, took items they shouldn't have, or have left cumbersome items and trash behind. That said, I would also have at the ready, the number of a scrap metal guy and/or junk removal service so you can present an immediate solution at the walk-through if need be.

If you expect the tenants/sellers to be problematic, I would arrive at the property early. If they have yet to vacate, call the listing agent and let them know the situation – that you will not be entering the home and will return with your buyers once that agent assures you it is vacant. Then call your buyers and explain the situation. If they are overly anxious, remind them that the opportunity for theft or damage (be it intentional or unintentional) is too great to accept the property at this time.

Another concern for a buyers' agent is repairs not having been completed or done well. Assuming your repair negotiations required licensed and insured professions to complete all repairs prior to the final walk-through, you should have been collecting paid receipts and having the items re-inspected as needed. The final walk-through is *not* the time to be confirming repairs have been made.

Conduct the final walk-through as if visiting the home for the first time. Walk the entire property and inspect all structures thoroughly. Check for:

o   Damaged walls, cracked floor tiles, dented door frames (from moving)

o   Damaged doorstops, porch stairs, driveway (from moving)

o   Doors and windows still open, close and lock

- Appliances in working order

- Toilets flush, faucets run hot and cold

- Heat and air-conditioning work

- All prior occupants' belongings are removed

- All items that should have been left are present

- Carpets are free of new stains

- No garbage is left in the home or on property

- Pool equipment turns on

- In-ground sprinklers turn on

If a small issue is found, be the problem solver and keep the buyers' emotions at bay. If it's something simple like mover scuff marks on a wall, go get the Magic Eraser® you keep in your car and try to take care of it. If it's bags of household trash and they fit in your trunk, cart them away.

If something of true concern is found at this late stage, it is always best to *go for a credit* rather than a repair. How much of a credit will need to be negotiated between the two parties, but often will require a professional to come out to quote the work. That said, if you did the walk-through on the way to closing, you will have no choice but to extend the closing. If however you had done it the morning prior, you just might get lucky enough to find a contractor to come out and quote the same day, allowing you to finalize negotiations without having to push back the closing.

Do note, if the sellers are leasing back the property from the buyers, and therefore will be remaining in the property after closing, you will have to conduct the walk-through with their contents present. In order to protect your buyers from any damage that may occur by the former owners after closing (or the possibility that they should not vacate the property on the expected date and your new buyers would need to evict), you must have an attorney draft a full lease. Buyers and sellers who have gotten friendly will occasionally talk about lease-back and believe it can be done with a simple handshake. Firmly explain to your buyers (put this in an email so you have proof of your correspondence) that you *strongly* advise *against* such a casual agreement and direct them to an attorney to further discuss the possible ramifications of not protecting themselves with a lease.

- **Closings**

  Prior to closing, reconfirm with your buyers the scheduled time, date, and location. Make certain the spouse (if any) will be present and that both bring their state issued driver's licenses with them. Moreover, check that they have/will send the wire and they have been provided the final closing amount and wire instructions.

  Just like the sellers' agent, you must be present in case something goes wrong at the closing. Be a calming presence, kill wait times by talking about their decorating plans for the new home, and keep your buyers calm by problem solving if a situation arises.

  Be prepared by bringing with you your full paper file, contact information for all parties that worked the transaction (the mortgage broker, the insurance broker, the home inspector, the attorney), and snacks for buyers' children. If you were required to obtain an original approval from a property association, remember to bring this and provide it to the closer.

Keep in Constant Communication with Your Buyers

Communications with buyers during the home search phase is different than during the contract phase. Initially, your responsiveness to showing requests and willingness to share what your research revealed on the different properties is what will please buyers. Once under contract, buyers are looking for the agent to convey updates quickly, keep them organized through deadline and appointment reminders, and spend time in person or on the phone problem solving with the buyers when issues arise. Of course, you will never touch base less than agreed upon in the Client/Agent Communications Expectations form.

From the qualifying meeting until the day after closing, make a point to call, email, and/or text your buyers – often.

NEW CONSTRUCTION BUYER REPRESENTATION

An agent would be wise to include new home construction buyer representation in their business model. New construction communities, which may consist of hundreds, even thousands, of single-family or multifamily homes when completed, offer excellent opportunities for agents.

Commissions on new construction tend to be on the higher end of market average, and occasionally a bonus will be offered. Time required of an agent for a new home transaction is less than one would spend on closing a resale home. The on-site builder representatives do the bulk of the agent's work. Moreover, when issues or delays arise *the builder representative breaks the bad news to your clients*, eliminating a potential source of contention in your client/agent relationship.

New construction home inspections typically pass, or, if issues are found the builder quickly remedies the defects. As such, the agent has peace of mind that the deal should not fall apart due to inspection issues – a threat to many resale transactions.

Defects in the home identified after occupancy are likely be remedied, or are required to be remedied, by either the builder or product manufacturers' warranties, quickly appeasing buyers. Similar defects identified after occupancy in a resale home would require the buyers to pay for repairs, possibly angering the buyers and triggering an accusation for agent liability regarding undisclosed conditions. The existence of builder and manufacturer warranties helps maintain positive client/agent relationships and lessen agent liability.

New construction, more often than not, appeals to the following buyers:

- **Perfectionists tend to embrace new construction.** You'll know you are dealing with a perfectionist after you have shown your buyers the best homes in the area that firmly meet their criteria, only to have one or both of them quickly reject house after house for insignificant reasons. Once you identify a perfectionist, save your sanity and make an appointment at a new construction home center.

  Professionally staged model homes, in which every upgrade has been added and every detail has been attended to, strongly resonate with perfectionists. National home builders spend an inconceivable amount of money testing which designs, materials, and features should go into their homes to attract the most buyers. And it shows. Bring a perfectionist to a model home and watch their eyes light up.

- **Buyers who fear purchasing "money pits" or find the idea of home maintenance overwhelming find new construction comforting.** Knowing that everything from the foundation to the roof is brand new gives these buyers' peace of mind.

  New construction often comes with a "1/2/10" warranty. This warranty insures up to one year for workmanship and materials, up to two years for systems within the home, such as electrical, plumbing, and HVAC, and up to ten years for major structural defects. Make certain to research if your state requires builders to provide warranties with a minimum amount of coverage or different time periods from above. Moreover, your state may have rules set in place as to how and when homeowners must report defects in order for claims to be paid. Keep in mind, builders warranties typically do **not** cover:

  o Homeowner abuse or neglect to maintain materials;

  o Damage caused by "acts of God," repairmen, or guests;

  o Appliances (stove, dryer, etc.), although, new appliances should be covered by manufacturer's warranties.

- **New construction can be a solution for frustrated buyers who have been searching in an area with limited resale home inventory.** Buyers may initially avoid new construction because they do not wish to wait out the build time. However, if buyers are losing home after home to other bidders in a tight market, or expect to have to wait a significant amount of time for a home that meets their criteria to come on the market, they may agree to consider new construction.

Representing Your Clients in New Construction

First and foremost, if you plan to work with new construction buyers you must become knowledgeable regarding new construction in your area:

- **Research the builders' reputations.**

   Conduct an online search for any complaints or bad reviews. Check if they are in good standing with the Better Business Bureau.

   Find out if the builder has completed any developments in your locale. Such information can usually be obtained on the builder websites or with a phone call to the sales office. If the builder has additional developments, determine if the communities have kept their value and desirability over the years. A comparison of the average price per square foot and time on market the development is currently experiencing against suitable comparables outside the community should be telling. If you don't have any personal experience with the homes, find a REALTOR® actively selling in the development through an MLS search. Explain why you are researching the community and any professional REALTOR® should be willing to share what they have learned during their transactions regarding general condition of homes, if not more. Also, visit the builder's older, completed communities and try to speak with a few homeowners. Ask questions in regards to their experience with the builder, the quality of their homes and level of satisfaction with the community as a whole. Some examples include:

   o   How has their home held up through the years?

o   Did the builder honor their warranties if any defect arose?

o   Were the amenities consistent with what homebuyers were promised and were they completed in a timely manner?

- **Meet with sales representatives; tour the models, amenities, and development.**

This is best accomplished by setting an appointment with a sales representative as opposed to just dropping in unannounced at the sales center. An appointment guarantees the sales person will have time to answer your questions. During your appointment you will also be trying to decide if the sales rep would be one you would be comfortable having your clients work with. Do they communicate effectively? Do they present themselves professionally? Are they knowledgeable about the building process, construction materials, etc.? Ideally, you will have *one sales rep at each development* that you can rely on to alert you to any incentives the builder is currently running, accept phone-in registrations from you (if within builder policy), and to treat your clients with care and respect. Keep in mind, new construction sales reps come in contact with unrepresented buyers on an almost daily basis. Make a point to *always* bring your buyers to the representative you befriend *and* remain professional, helpful, and respectful during the transactions. You just might find the builder's sales person becomes an excellent referral source – sending those unrepresented buyers who did not care for their development to you.

Ask the sales rep to provide you with:

- Standard floor plans and their base price;

- Plat of the lots with current pricing;

- A list of proposed amenities and their planned locations;

- Any brochures or marketing materials for the community;

- A list of upgrades and design choices.

Questions to ask the sales rep:

- When is the last home expected to be completed?

- How many lots are currently available?

- Which lots are more desirable/higher in cost?

- Do options or upgrades require deposits or pre-payments on top of the earnest money deposit?

- Are additional phases planned?

- What is the typical build time?

- Are there any current buyer incentives?

- When is the builder's fiscal year end?

- Is FHA and/or VA financing possible in the community?

- Is, or will, the community be gated or have a security patrol?

- Is there a mandatory homeowner association fee? Is it paid monthly, quarterly, annually? What does it pay for?

- Is there an available list of rules and regulations home-owners will be required to follow?

- Is the sales rep a licensed REALTOR®, and thus bound to the NAR's Code of Ethics and Standards of Practice?

After your questions are answered, request a tour of the model homes. If the rep is willing, ask them to conduct the tour as if you were a buyer. Experience the sales presentation from a buyer's per-spective. You'll likely pick up a few talking points that may sway re-luctant buyers to visit the development and eliminate any surprises when you accompany buyers on a tour.

Do not forget to ask to tour any amenities under construction or completed. If the builder has yet to break ground or complete the amenities, ask to see any paperwork the rep may have that requires the amenities to be built to any specific criteria. Be aware, amenities are often *not guaranteed* in the purchase contracts.

Walk or drive the streets. Are any streets cul-de-sacs? Are there sidewalks? How closely are the homes situated? Are they positioned on the front or rear of the lots? Are mailboxes individual to the homes or in groupings? Try to get a gauge as to the different locations/sizes of the premium vs. standard lots.

- **Before leaving, ask the sales representative to send you a copy of their purchase contract and review copy of any warranties that accompany the homes.**

Builders typically *require* their purchase contracts to be used. The sales representative should be able to email you a copy of their contract. Read through it carefully. After digesting, reach back out to the sales rep with any questions you may have. Some items that often need clarification include:

- o Is this, in fact, the only purchase contract the builder will accept? This will typically be the case, and the contract will likely be more favorable to the builder than the buyers.

- o Do the buyers have a window for attorney review? If not, provide your offer to your clients' attorney *before* submitting it to the builder.

- o Can the contract be marked up? The builder may not accept offers with strikethroughs or additions.

- o Can the buyers' escrow their deposits with their attorney? If so, is there a fee to the builder to do so? It is common that escrow monies are put into the builders' operating accounts. With an established builder, your clients might be comfortable with such an arrangement; some, however, may not be.

o Can the buyers visit the site during construction, and can they select their own independent home inspector? If so, when are inspections allowed? Ideally you would want the inspector to be allowed to access the site three to four times during the build.

o What protections do buyers have under the cost clause? Builders use the clause to protect against labor and material shortages resulting in cost increases, interest rate hikes etc., stating they have the right to charge the buyers for such and the buyers in turn have the right to pay or cancel the contract. You want to understand if your buyers' right to cancel includes the return of their deposit, if increases are capped at a certain amount, and/or if they are compensated in such an instance.

o If the contract does not include wording for paying the agent, get a copy of the builders' commission policy. Are agents paid commission solely on the base price or on base *plus* options?

o What do the warranties cover and how are issues remedied?

New Construction Showings

Always attend tours with your buyers. Some builders will not honor your commission if you do not accompany your buyers on their first visit. Schedule them ahead of time with your preferred sales center representative.

Once you arrive, introduce your clients to the representative and then take a respectful backseat to their interactions. Let the rep lead the tour and answer all questions. Respect that they are more knowledgeable about the homes then you are. Never talk over the rep or try to discredit the rep in any way. This is not the time to act possessive about your buyers. If at the end you believe the rep has failed to discuss something that you know your clients would weigh heavily in their decision making process, lead the conversation in that direction.

Do not try to negotiate price with the sales rep during showings. In regards to pricing, showings are the time to discern between what is standard and what are upgrades as you walk through the models.

New Construction Pricing and Negotiations

Most homebuyers assume new construction and resale home purchase negotiations would be the same. Nothing could be further from the truth.

Resale negotiations are typically focused on getting the purchase price as low as possible. One goes about saving clients' money on new construction differently.

Contrary to public belief, builders do not make a large profit on each home. Developments are a numbers game. There is huge overhead with a very thin profit margin on each home. Those thin margins have to add up to create any true profit for the builder, thus the large numbers of homes built at once. They make money on upgrades.

Help your buyers take advantage of builder offered incentives. Keep on top of any current or likely future incentives through communications with the sales reps. Note that incentives are more common close to the builder's fiscal year end.

Negotiate and advise on upgrades – don't haggle over the model base price. This will frustrate many buyers, so you will need to educate them as to why this can be a positive negotiation. The vast majority of builders do not want to veer from the base price as it would result in driving down the value of the next homes they build. Purchase prices are public record. Instead of knocking $5,000 off the base price, the builders would rather give an extra $5,000 in physical upgrades (for instance, installing granite instead of laminate on bathroom vanities). That negotiation would never be seen by appraisers or future buyers, who could use a reduced model base price as a comparable to force the builders to discount future home sale prices. With upgrade negotiations, your clients receive something of value and peace of mind that the development values will not be forced down. This home is an investment for them too; they wouldn't want it to appraise any lower than necessary in the future either.

Another way to help your clients save money in the long run is to offer to be present when they visit the design center and advise them on their upgrade selections. Some will not want you present and that's okay. However, if they do wish you to attend, try to steer them towards a safer alternative should they veer towards styles or products that you know would be detrimental from a resale perspective. Choosing something very personal to their tastes (shiny purple and gold kitchen cabinets) would limit the future buyer pool, potentially costing them an unnecessarily long time on market and likely price reductions. Too over-the-top upgrades (recessed wall espresso machine) will probably not get them any return on their money. Under-improvements should also be brought to their attention. If they start leaning towards vinyl kitchen flooring in a million dollar home, you should gently explain that future buyers would not find that product acceptable in such a price point. Your personal preferences should not be expressed; your professional knowledge should be shared – and hopefully they take your insights into consideration. One word of caution, if your buyers are using financing to purchase the home, you will need to be more firm about keeping their selections in check. *Their financing, and therefore your deal, could be jeopardized if their choices push the price over appraised value.* Some buyers have the ability to bring more money to the table; in that event, if the upgrades are important enough to them they will pay for them. For those who don't have additional funds, you will have to make certain they do not over-improve the home.

Another way to help your buyers save money is to encourage them to buy sooner than later. Many buyers want the development to be near completion before they buy in. They would feel more comfortable surrounded by neighbors, would have to endure less construction noise, and would have completed amenities to enjoy. Those are all valid points, and the builder recognizes them as such by raising home prices as more homes are completed. Convey to your clients that the earlier they buy into a development, the better deal they will typically receive. Plus, they will have more lots to choose from.

While not part of negotiations, per se, you can greatly decrease your clients' costs by *stressing that they limit their change orders to as few as possible.* Get them in the mindset to firmly decide on as many details as possible before signing. Change orders are costly (requiring pre-payments, fees, and/or penalties) and increase the build time. If they do make change orders, stress that they always get them in writing and provide you with a copy so you can also help confirm they have all been completed prior to close.

New Construction Closing Considerations

First and foremost, stress to your buyers that title insurance should be obtained on new construction. People often wrongly believe that since the parcel was previously unimproved, there is no need for title insurance. Encumbrances, liens, title defects – everything that title insurance is meant to protect against – can, and does, happen on farmland and vacant land. Protect your clients; always have them obtain title insurance.

The home is rarely 100% complete during the final walk-through. Builders work up to closing (and commonly after) to finish the final details. For instance, landscaping is typically dropped in the day of closing. This eliminates the builders from ever having to pay for watering, mowing, fertilizing, etc. Regardless, schedule your walk-through as close to closing as possible. You, your buyers, the sales rep, and the construction representative should all attend the walk-through. The home inspector should have already been through and if he noted anything that needed repair, you will include it on the "punch list." The "punch list" documents items the builder still needs to repair, add, or complete. Take your time with your buyers in the home. Do not let the builder representatives rush you. Bring *all* change orders to double check all work has been completed. If not completed, add it to the list. Look at everything and consider every single component of the item. For example, when inspecting a bedroom closet ask yourself:

- Are these the closet doors the buyers selected?
- Do the closet doors look aligned?
- Do they slide smoothly on the track?
- Are the door knobs attached?
- Are they the door knobs the buyers selected?
- Are the doors painted on both sides?
- Is the paint a top coat or just primer?

And that's just one closet door... Everyone in attendance should sign the punch list. Make certain to get a copy for your file. You do not want your buyers to "trust" that the builder will complete the list after closing. If items appear on the punch list that would prove upsetting to your clients if never corrected, either push back the closing date or negotiate to have a portion of the purchase price held in escrow after closing until the punch list has been completed.

Lastly, be diligent about making sure an affidavit of No Liens is provided to the buyers from the builder. If the builder fails to pay subcontractors from the build, a construction lien could be filed holding your buyers responsible for payment. I would strongly suggest having an attorney review the affidavit, and if one is not provided seek the attorney's advice on the matter.

After Closing

Keep providing value after closing. Remind buyers to schedule their home inspector to revisit (or inspect for the first time if they were not contractually allowed on-site during the build) a month or two prior to their home warranty expiration. Issues found should be resolved while still under warranty, possibly saving them hundreds if not thousands of dollars. Moreover, each year on their closing anniversary, send them a CMA (if their home has appreciated in value). It's a warm touch and everyone loves hearing they made a good financial decision.

Agents Beware

New construction should always be discussed during your initial buyers' consultation with new clients. At minimum, you must impress upon them the value of having you represent them, and in order for you to do so they must allow you to accompany them on their first visit or give you time to properly register them with the builder at *every* community they may be interested in. Remember, many registrations expire. Keep copies of the registration and never fail to re-register your clients on-time.

Another threat to your commission is new construction homes listed on the MLS. Just because a builder has a MLS listing you are not fully protected on your commission. Your commission *is only protected when your buyers purchase the exact home/lot listed on the MLS*. Always, no matter what, register your clients immediately when arriving at new construction communities. If your buyers choose to purchase a different model or lot, and you have failed to register them with the builder, you will have learned a very expensive lesson – the hard way.

RENTALS

Rentals... agents seem to either love 'em or hate 'em. Regardless, every agent must make a business decision whether to take 'em or leave 'em.

There are rental agents who build their businesses exclusively around lease transactions.

The low commission to be had on rentals is remedied by the high volume agents can churn. Their singular focus allows them to become extremely efficient with the leasing process and proficient with the forms. Rentals close quickly so agents can enjoy a steady income stream.

Newly licensed agents and struggling agents might find dedicating two years to heavily working rentals a highly strategic move for their business. Why?

1. The learning curve is shortened. Initially, the agent need only become proficient with the leasing contract and forms. Moreover, inventory is more uniform and therefore, unit floorplans and building amenities are able to be memorized faster.

2. Commissions can be had in weeks as opposed to months. Since leasing transactions close quickly, rentals can alleviate financial pressures the agent might be experiencing.

3. Advertising costs to find landlords and renters is minimal, if not free. Social media and Craigslist have proven successful outlets for advertising.

4. In a very short time, the agent will have a large pipeline of leads and clients. Moreover, numerous transactions should result in numerous client testimonials the agent can use in their marketing efforts.

5. After the first year, assuming they did a good job *and kept in touch*, landlords will relist and tenants will ask the agent to help them find their next rental.

6. After one year the agent will also start enjoying renewal commissions. Renewal commissions are paid by *some* landlords when a lease is renewed by the same tenants for another term. Renewal commissions are basically "free money," as no additional work is required on the part of the agent to collect.

7. After one or two years, the agent will find their previous tenants are now ready to buy their own homes. If the agent had provided a positive rental experience, and made a point *to stay in touch and build a relationship with the tenants over the years*, most likely the tenants will choose to be represented by the agent when purchasing a home.

   A wise agent will always ask tenants if their future dreams involve purchasing a home. If they indicate an interest in homeownership, the agent should dedicate time to become a resource for them. Mortgage broker referrals should be provided. The agent will explain the benefits of meeting with a mortgage broker *long before* they are ready to buy so they can better assess what credit issues they need to remedy, when they are likely to be approved for a loan, and for how much. The agent will also send them occasional market updates and make themselves available to answer any questions tenants might have about the buying process. *Educate tenants, and they will be buyers – sooner.*

8. Once the agent starts servicing previous tenants-turned-buyers, they should find themselves in an excellent position to either expand or shift their business if they so desire. The agent may want to create a team or bring on a partner so as to keep feeding and servicing the rentals while also branching into sales. The agent may prefer to slow the amount of rentals and increase the amount of sales he or she works. Either way the earlier years of rental work should have built the agent a sustainable and successful business.

There are sales agents who do not accept landlords or tenants as clients.

Refusing to work rentals may purely be a business decision for busy agents. In Florida, where all commissions are negotiable, a single side of a rental transaction tends to fall around half of one month's rent. One side of a sale commission typically pays between 2.5 and 3% of the contract sale price. As such, rental and sale commissions are likely thousands if not tens of thousands of dollars apart. Time is a limited resource. A busy agent will not give up precious hours to service a rental when he or should could be working with sellers or buyers.

Refusing to service tenants and landlords may also be an emotional decision for an agent. It does not take long working rentals to learn how frustrating the experience can be. It takes a strong agent to set proper expectations, and for lack of a better word, "control" their clients.

Most agents include rentals in the mix of services they provide their clients – even if they don't advertise working rentals.

Ask an agent if they like working rentals, and you'll likely get one of two responses similar to the following:

1. "Rentals are the bane of my existence."

2. "Rentals pay my rent."

The first response, "Rentals are the bane of my existence," speaks to the frustration many agents experience while working rentals. First time renters often have unrealistic expectations and require a lot of hand holding. Long-term renters can have time-consuming hurdles, such as bad credit, multiple pets, or criminal records that require extra time for hard searches and pitching to landlords to accept them. Moreover, renters tend to behave more like headaches than clients, often stopping communication suddenly or juggling multiple agents at once. Landlords can also prove problematic. Typical examples include landlords wanting agents to illegally screen tenants with disregard to protected classes as defined by HUD's Fair Housing Act, asking outrageous rents, or failing to clean and/or make needed repairs to the property prior to the tenants' move-in date.

The second response, "Rentals pay my rent," seems to be the most common sentiment among agents. Rentals provide money to offset overhead costs, not to make them rich. If a rental drops in their lap, they'll take it. If one of their buyers or sellers needs a temporary rental, they will make it happen. If they hit a slow patch they might seek out a rental or two to plug a hole in their production; rentals are a bit of a necessary evil. However, they would be unlikely to spend advertising money to find renters to service.

WORKING WITH TENANTS

Working with tenants is similar in many ways to working with buyers. It always feels good to find someone their new home. Typically, the time spent with renters is less than that with buyers, but hours spent in showings does allow for a true relationship to form. Always remember, today's tenants might be next year's buyers, so always work professionally, provide excellent service, and remember to keep in touch throughout the years!

Your Obligations to Tenants

You owe your tenants patience, strength, competency, and attention. Just like buyers, they hired a professional to find them a home in their criteria that they can afford. If you plan to treat them as an afterthought simply because their transaction will not garner you as much commission as a sale, you need to refer them to another agent that will give them the attention they deserve.

Qualify Tenants – Always

Always, always, always qualify tenants. There is not enough money to be made on a rental to spend unnecessary time and gas showing the wrong properties.

Like buyers, set a time to meet with potential tenants *before* showing properties. If they refuse to meet with you, do not work with them. You will conduct the qualifying meeting similar to when qualifying buyers to their desired home criteria and price range. However, there are a few additional tenant specific questions you will want to ask:

- Who will be occupying the property? If more than one person, how many are over 18? Alert them to the fact that anyone over the age of 18 will be expected to appear on the lease and all credit and background checks required by landlords or associations will likely be run on every adult.

- Do you have any pets? If so, what kind and how many? Dogs require you to know breed and weight. If they have cats ask if they are declawed and/or neutered/spayed.

- Are they smokers? If so, do they smoke inside?

- How many vehicles do they have? Is there commercial signage on any of the vehicles? If they have trucks, what size are they? Many communities do not allow trucks or commercial vehicles.

- Do they need any physical accommodations?

- How long would they like to lease for?

- What is their current living situation? How long have they been at that address? How soon would they like to move? You must educate them as to when it is best for them to start looking based on your specific market.

- How is their credit? When was the last time it was run? If they know their credit to be poor, do they have someone with good credit willing to co-sign for them? If they do not know their score, suggest they run their annual free credit report and provide you with their numbers thereafter.

- Are they currently employed? If so, for how long?

- Will a criminal background check result in any convictions that might make the landlords question their other tenants' safety or protection of their property?

- Have they ever been evicted?

- Do they intend to have guests stay for extended periods? If so, for how long?

Needless to say, depending on how the above are answered, you may have a few issues to work around. That is to be expected with tenants. If their problems happened years ago, have the tenants write a letter to present to landlords which explains that they have not had any issues since. If they have poor credit, ask their permission to see if the landlords will accept them if they put down a larger deposit or pay some months upfront. If they have an old eviction, suggest they ask their current landlords for a letter of recommendation. Problem solved, that's what you are hired for.

Respect the Tenants' Time

Conduct home searches, showings, and negotiations in the same professional way you work with buyers.

Preparing Offers

Before preparing an offer, always call the listing agent to make sure the rental has not gone under contract. Rentals move fast.

When preparing the offer, regardless of what form you use, make certain it hits on all terms important to your tenants from a negotiation standpoint. Monthly rent, refundable and non-refundable deposits, lease start and end dates, what utilities and maintenance they are willing to pay should all be within the offer. Additionally, if the tenants refuse to move in until it is cleaned, make certain to write this into the offer. For instance, "Landlords agree to have the unit professionally cleaned prior to lease commencement." If something is important to your tenants, get it into the offer. You should know your rental market enough to help guide them as to what and how much negotiation is likely to end in their securing the rental vs. losing the rental.

In Florida, our offers are drafted on *Contract to Lease* forms which outline the typically negotiated terms. While it is a legally binding document once signed by all parties, it is primarily used to get through the negotiations and as a blueprint for an attorney to work off of when drafting the actual lease, which will spell out in detail both the tenants' and landlords' obligations and penalties. Once the lease is signed, it supersedes the *Contract to Lease*.

Review the Lease

Typically, landlords will have the lease drafted. Once the lease is received, take the time to read through it carefully *before* presenting it to your tenants for signature.

Your state bar and/or REALTOR® association may have a standard residential lease for agents to prepare. Attorneys and landlords can also draft leases. As such, you will be presented with numerous, if not hundreds, of different leases during your career. Be aware, a lease prepared by the other side will likely contain a large number of terms that *favor the landlords*.

The only way to protect your tenants is to comb through *each line and item by item* searching for drafting errors and unfavorable terms or conditions. Identified drafting errors should be brought to the landlords' agent's attention. Terms or conditions that appear unfavorable for your tenants should be discussed between you and your clients and then negotiated with the other side. Keep in mind, should the landlords not be willing to negotiate one or more of the terms your tenants will have to make the decision to accept the terms or find another property to lease. Once landlord and tenants come to an agreement, the lease should be corrected accordingly, *prior to your tenants signing*.

- **Check for preparer errors or omissions by making certain:**

  All parties' names are properly spelled

  Landlord matches the name or legal entity on the property deed

  The property address is correct and complete with unit number

  Lease term is correct (start and end dates). If the length of term triggers additional requirements, are those requirements present? For example, in Florida, a lease written for longer than one year triggers a two witness signature requirement.

  Monthly installments, security deposits, and charges are the negotiated upon dollar amounts

If the lease term is imperfect, the straggler days appear on the lease and are accurately prorated at a daily rate

Taxes (short-term rentals may trigger a tourist tax) appear with the correct dollar amount or percentage and the correct party is indicated as responsible for payment

Non-tenant occupants (minors, part-time occupants) are listed and are properly spelled

Deposits and fees (such as pet deposits or cleaning fees) are clearly written as either refundable or non-refundable

The proper party is noted as responsible for each utility (electric, gas, water, cable, etc.)

The correct party is indicated as responsible for maintenance and/or repair for any applicable items on the Property (landscaping, plumbing, extermination, appliances, etc.)

The correct breeds, weights, and number of pets (if any) are noted in the lease

The financial institution in which the tenants' security deposit is to be escrowed is identified in the lease

- **Evaluate the terms and conditions through your Tenants' perspective:**

Are the late payment fees excessive?

Does the lease protect the tenants' right for "quiet enjoyment?" "Quiet enjoyment" within a lease protects tenants from more than noise level; it encompasses their rights to enjoy the property without unnecessary disturbances as long as they are following the law and lease terms. Any condition that allows for your tenants to be disturbed during their occupancy should be discussed with your tenants. For example, a lease might state that if the property is placed for sale, the tenants must accommodate showings. Some tenants would have no problem with the possibility of prospective buyers traipsing through their home. Others would be incensed by it. If your clients are the latter, negotiations must take place. Perhaps the landlords will be willing to remove the condition completely? A middle ground may be found by altering the verbiage to only allow showings in the last month of the lease or restricting the showings to certain times/dates, etc. If it is a condition that is very important to the landlords, perhaps a reduction in rent could be negotiated for the tenants' cooperation with showings.

If the tenants are smokers, does the lease clearly permit or prohibit smoking on the premises?

Are tenants' repair obligations clearly defined? Repairs should be capped at a specific dollar amount *for the duration of the lease*. If the lease states the tenants are responsible for "repairs under $100 dollars," that is too vague for interpretation and you should advise your tenants of such. On the surface it seems like a minimal amount. However, without verbiage to limit it to no more than $100 in repairs *for the duration of the lease*, your clients will be on the hook for possibly much more. What if one problematic appliance broke on numerous occasions? What if multiple appliances break over the course of the lease? Either scenario could quickly add up to hundreds of dollars your clients would be contractually obligated to pay.

Are pre-occupancy landlords' obligations included in the lease? Any promises the landlords made regarding professional cleaning, repairs, and/or improvements to the property that your tenants are expecting to happen prior to occupancy must be written into the lease. Otherwise, your tenants will have no recourse if the landlords fail to honor their word. Such obligations should be clearly spelled out with a definitive required date of completion, allowing the tenants to inspect the work has been done satisfactorily prior to lease start. Unless your state laws proves to be the exception, *a lease will take precedence over earlier executed agreements* between the landlords and tenants, such as a *Contract to Lease*, term sheets, or offers to lease. Therefore, if the pre-occupancy promises are present in earlier agreements, but do not appear in the lease, your tenants will not be protected.

If there is assigned parking, is the stall or space number indicated on the lease?

Has a copy of your state's Landlord-Tenant Laws been provided to your tenants prior to lease signing? If this is not a state mandate, it would still be prudent practice to provide one to all your tenants. Make certain you have read and understand it – of great import is to note which landlord-tenant laws cannot be overridden via lease or contract terms.

If the structure is older than 1978, does a lead-based paint disclosure completed by the landlords accompany the lease? Have the landlords provided the Environmental Protection Agency pamphlet *Protect Your Family From Lead In Your Home*, or your state approved pamphlet?

If the property is governed by a homeowner or condominium owner association which requires tenants to be approved, is there a clause releasing your tenants from the lease if they were to be denied?

Does the lease provide a large enough window of time to accommodate any out-of-town guest your tenants expect to house?

Moving the Tenants In

Once the lease is signed by all parties, the association approval, if any, is received, and the pre-occupancy deposits have been collected, you pretty much will just be waiting for the move-in date.

At least three days prior to move-in, supply your tenants with a list of providers they will need to contact to get the utilities switched over to their names by lease start.

Schedule a time with the listing agent for you and your tenants to meet with them at the property for the walk-through and key exchange. Bring a property inspection sheet (in case the listing agent fails to provide one) for your clients to mark down any existing conditions on the property at the time. Holes in walls, dents in appliances, carpet stains, basically anything that they want to be sure their security deposit is not jeopardized over. Have your tenants sign and date the form and provide to the listing agent for landlords to sign. Instruct your clients to also document the items with dated photographs or video.

Once condition is documented, and any monies due are handed to the listing agent, tenants should receive the keys to the unit.

Remember to keep in touch with your tenants. At worst, they are another rental in a year. At best, they may become buyers. Let them know you are always available to discuss things they can be doing now to help them buy in the future.

WORKING WITH LANDLORDS

Working with landlords is very similar to taking a listing with home sellers. You want to make certain you are asking a fair price for their property and meeting your obligations as set forth in your rental listing agreement. You will negotiate your commission at the time of taking the listing. Do note, if legal in your state, you will also want to negotiate a new lease, renewal, or sale commission at the same time. This would ensure you being paid a commission if landlords create a new lease with, or renews the lease of, or even sells to tenants you were responsible for placing in their property.

Your Obligations to Landlords

- Know your rental market and base your suggested lease price off a carefully conducted CMA.

- Honor all terms in your *Right to Lease Agreement*.

- Work hard to effectively market the property.

- Learn any leasing rules, regulations, approval requirements and amount of time approvals take as dictated by a governing association, if applicable.

- Create an accurate and descriptive MLS Listing. Refer back to your listing agreement to double check which utilities and maintenance the landlords are willing to pay for.

Educate Landlords

Discuss disclosures with landlords early on. Lead-based paint disclosure *does apply to rentals* and landlords are required to report any knowledge of lead paint and provide an Environmental Protection Agency pamphlet, *Protect Your Family From Lead In Your Home*, or your state-approved pamphlet.

Although likely included in your listing agreement, always firmly explain to your landlords that *under no circumstances* will you deny renting the landlords' property to anyone of a protected class, be it state or federal. If any landlords are not willing to abide by the law, cancel the listing.

Learn how your state requires landlords to hold security deposits and make certain your landlords are able to comply. For example, Florida requires the monies to be kept in a Florida financial institution. Out-of-state landlords appreciate being notified of the rule at the time of the listing so they can set up an in-state account before any deposit monies are in play, and you get to avoid last minute headaches.

Have your landlords contact their insurance agent to make certain their current policy will work with tenants in place. If the landlords are providing the unit furnished, have them alert their insurance broker of such. Suggest your landlords require their tenants to carry a renter's policy for the duration of the lease, on which they are to name the landlords as additionally insured.

Presenting Offers to Landlords

Local customs and what was dictated in your listing agreement will determine what you provide to your landlords for their review above and beyond prospective tenants' offers. They may ask you to pull prospective tenants' credit, run background checks, and have tenants fill out applications and/or present proof of income and employment. Make sure you follow all laws when acquiring such information. Your broker will likely have policies in place to help you.

Preparing the Lease

Once negotiations have ended, it is usually the landlords, landlords' attorney, or landlords' agent who prepares the lease (if legal in your state). For example, in Florida, agents are only allowed to prepare leases, no longer than one-year in duration, on the state prescribed form. In my opinion, landlords should always opt to have their attorney (or one recommended by you) prepare the lease. For very little cost, you remove liability from yourself and your brokerage, and your landlords will likely receive a lease that protects them better than any generic state prescribed lease would.

If the unit is to be rented furnished, create a list of contents to be included as an attachment to the lease. Take your time, break down contents per room, and be descriptive. Include serial and model numbers when applicable. Take photographs of expensive items and include them with the attachment. The contents list should be referred to within the lease and signed and dated by all parties.

Once the attorney-drafted lease is returned and before you present it to your landlords for signatures, you should double check that all the agreed upon terms were correctly included and that no errors in regard to names, dates, etc. are present. Lawyers are human too.

Once signed by your landlords, provide to the other side for signatures. Make certain any pre-occupancy tenants' deposits are collected in the form of cashier's check or money order, so funds are guaranteed, and deposited as directed in the lease.

At lease start, be present when the tenants document the property condition. Their completed and signed condition report should be forwarded to your landlords for signatures and then returned. If you were to collect rent or monies at the key exchange forward this to your landlords as well.

A word of caution: **NEVER** let tenants take possession of a unit prior to association approval. If they are denied, you'll have an unenforceable lease and likely a problem removing them from the property. If tenants wish to take possession of the property before the lease begins but do have association approval or one is not needed, *still* strongly advise the landlords against it without having an addendum to the lease drawn up to cover landlords for any liability or situation that may arise. Check your state laws as to who can legally draft an addendum to a signed lease (it is illegal for an agent to do so in Florida). Lastly, do not allow tenants to store possessions on the property before lease start without an addendum removing liability for the contents from the landlords. Too often, kind landlords accept tenants' request for one of the above situations only to horribly regret it just a few short days later.

WORKING REFERRALS

After listings, referrals provide an amazing revenue stream. Any licensed agents in the U.S., or abroad, are a possible referral source. Remember, referral commissions are negotiable.

Forming relationships with out-of-locale agents increases your likelihood for incoming referrals. Interact with out-of-locale agents on social media. Make a point to meet agents while traveling, reach out via phone or email to agents in your brokerage's other offices. You will be sharing your commission with the referring agent, but you will have spent neither money (advertising) nor time (multiple touches) acquiring the client. A word of caution, I do not recommend accepting low-end rental referrals; you could lose money servicing them once the referral commission is paid. Remember like all commissions, referral commissions are negotiable.

Always keep the referring agent in the loop as to how transactions are moving along. I share updates in regards to contract signing when each contingency clears and when closing is to occur. They chose you with the expectations that you will first, treat their client as well as they would *and* second, get the deal done. One successful transaction typically results in future referrals. Treat referral transactions and all parties involved with great care.

In order to benefit from out-going referrals, you will have to educate your clients and spheres as to the fact they can, and why they would, *recommend you to people buying or selling out-of-area.* "The best compliment I could receive is your referral." Perhaps that is written on your own business card or email signature? This common phrase, while it might bring you some local incoming referrals, completely misses the mark for the opportunity for out-going ones. The average person reading that statement would assume the agent is asking to be told if they know of anyone in the immediate area that has a real estate need. As stated before, you need to *educate* people regarding out-going referrals and that cannot happen in one short sentence. Dedicate a paragraph to it every now and then in newsletters and touches. Bring it up lightly in phone conversations on occasion. "I'd love to help your out-of-area friends and family find an amazing agent in their locale. If they are thinking about buying or selling, while unfortunately I can't physically represent them, I am more than happy to interview a few agents for them that can. I know all the right insider questions to ask in order to separate the wheat from the chaff. I'm always happy to help provide a positive real estate experience for the important people in your life." Suddenly, they can see how they, and you, can provide true value to their distant friends and family.

Keep in mind that you may not actively participate in out-going referrals. Once you have a signed referral agreement, you may not provide advice or opinion on the relationship with the selected agent or the resulting transaction. Too often those clients will call you complaining about the agent once emotions come into play or asking you to look over the contract as a second set of eyes, etc. You must politely decline. You are *not* their agent, and it is therefore unethical to involve yourself in any way. If the referral is in a state you are not licensed in, you have neither an understanding of their practices nor laws, so it would be ridiculous to try to answer questions. Moreover, it would be *illegal*. You would be practicing real estate without a license, and possibly be practicing law without a license. Always direct the clients back to their referred agent or that agent's broker.

REAL ESTATE LAW

Dear Real Estate Agent,

No need to be afraid. No need to be intimidated.

I am a lawyer to help your clients. *I am a lawyer to help you.*

I am not here to create problems. *I solve problems.*

I don't default to cancelling transactions. *I focus on closing transactions.*

Who else can you and your clients lean on during a transaction? *I am here for you.*

I understand some lawyers may frustrate, even anger, rather than support real estate agents. However, strong and ethical attorneys always keep in the front of their mind the reason the clients signed the contract in the first place – they wanted to buy or sell a home. I feel accomplished when they see their goals brought to fruition.

Let me help you help them.

Sincerely,

Gregory R. Cohen, Esquire

REAL ESTATE LAW

As a real estate agent, you are called to represent sellers, buyers, land-lords, and tenants. They are entrusting you to handle the entire process and always look out for their best interests. Regardless of the documentation, whether you are a dual agent, transactional agent, or have no fiduciary obligation whatsoever, in their eyes, you are there to help, guide, and protect them. That said, ask yourself:

- Why not suggest your clients hire an attorney to be involved on their behalf, alongside you, so they are, in fact, fully represented?

- Why not have an attorney step in to absorb a large portion of the responsibility of protecting your clients and therefor relieve you of undue pressure and risk?

- Why not allow an attorney to focus on and handle the contractual details and other legal matters? Wouldn't your time be better spent tackling marketing, showings, attending due diligence inspections, coordinating all parties on the transaction, and client communications?

Regardless if you are licensed in a state or district that requires an attorney be involved in real estate transactions, or if it is optional in your locale, I need you to be informed as to the benefits, and know how to avoid the detriments. Further, I believe as a real estate agent you must be aware and mindful of the problems that frequently arise out of real estate transactions and an attorney is typically able to circumvent or resolve (e.g. contract issues and the unauthorized practice of law).

HELP YOUR CLIENTS FIND THE RIGHT (AND AVOID THE WRONG) ATTORNEY

Many real estate agents refer to attorneys as "deal killers"– a description that I cannot stand. However, I do understand why it persists. Just as an inexperienced, weak, part-time real estate agent can fail to keep a deal together, a sub-par attorney can "kill the deal." Sadly, many attorneys have earned the stigma. Some wrongly feel they are protecting their clients by accentuating all risks, which in effect, scares them into backing out of the deal. Others "bubble wrap" their clients' offers. These attorneys draft offers so heavily one-sided in their clients' benefit that the other party is insulted and will react by rejecting the first, and all too often, any later offers from them. Neither is an effective way for attorneys to represent clients, and both approaches are detrimental to transactions.

The most effective way for a real estate agent to control the experience both you and your clients will have with an attorney is to *make certain you are recommending strong, experienced ones for your clients to choose from.* Once the attorney is hired, you are obligated to complete the transaction alongside them. Of course, some clients come to you already having an attorney, in which case, you just have to hope for the best. However, for clients who have yet to hire legal representation, guiding them towards competent, local, full-time real estate attorneys is one of the best ways for you to ensure a successful close.

In locales where an attorney is not required, I am aware some agents attempt to keep attorneys out by intentionally minimizing an attorney's importance when they discuss their clients' right to obtain one (which might I add, I believe is a breach of your fiduciary obligation to them – and you may find yourself under review if the transaction goes south). These agents are only hurting themselves. Many clients will seek attorney representation on their own. The likelihood of clients selecting an inexperienced attorney, one out of the area, or one with an outrageous ego, will greatly increase if you (the agent who has to work through the entire transaction alongside the attorney) do not provide them with your list of carefully selected attorneys to choose from.

Keep in mind, when I say inexperienced I do not only mean a small amount of time under their belt practicing law. I also mean any attorney who has limited experience in real estate law. Regardless of how long they have been practicing, do not recommend an attorney who focuses their practice on family law and only dabbles in real estate law part-time. You should always recommend an attorney whose primary focus is real estate. Otherwise, commonplace industry issues can be new to them, and neither you nor your clients want the attorney learning on your time.

The same is true when considering the attorney's office location. When I say local, I don't mean only an attorney licensed in your state, but rather someone who lives and works full time in your area. Real estate law can be vastly different from state to state, but even customary practices (e.g. if sellers or buyers pays for title) can vary from county to county.

You'll know when you are dealing with a part-time or out-of-area attorney. They are the ones that question customary verbiage in the pre-printed contracts and forms. It is only on rare occasion that an attorney may have a pertinent issue to a specific client that would require altering prescribed verbiage. Before you know it, the inexperienced attorney is creating confusion and damage within the contract that will have to be undone. Standard verbiage is in the clients' best interest most of the time, as the preprinted forms were written to resolve common industry issues identified over the years – a full-time local real estate attorney would know exactly how and why the forms were written in the manner they were.

I see this a lot when dealing with New York attorneys on Florida documents. In New York, attorneys are heavily involved in the drafting and preparation of contracts. As a result, a New York attorney often reviews our Florida form contracts and usually provide one to two pages in additions and revisions. It then rests on me to undo the damage by explaining the common issues and practices in Florida so that nobody gets emotional, the contract gets signed, and everyone keeps their eyes on the ball. There are enough regular issues in a transaction. Why add to them by having your clients use an out-of-area attorney?

REAL ESTATE ATTORNEYS' OBJECTIVES

In order to ensure your clients will be properly represented, you must understand the different objectives experienced real estate attorneys strive to accomplish:

- **Effectuate the Clients' Goals**

The goal of a transaction is to sell and/or buy, and the attorney is there to effectuate that goal. The first purpose as an attorney is to effectuate the goals of the clients, whether they are buyers or sellers. The attorney ensures they are purchasing and selling as anticipated. In order to do that, the attorney's role is to review the contract, review and/or create the closing documents, advocate for the clients, and offer ideas to address issues that arise throughout transactions. The contract documents are to express their wishes so that there is no confusion, so that no problems arise, and so there is no loss of value to those clients. I have heard real estate agents argue that around 85% of the residential contracts are template verbiage and therefore not overly complicated for an agent to complete. However, they are underestimating how many issues can arise within the remaining 15% when left to the discretion of a non-attorney. When an effective and knowledgeable attorney draws up a contract themselves, or reviews one that has already been prepared *before* it is circulated, both you and your clients enjoy protections.

- **To Practice Law**

Does this seem too obvious? Unfortunately, some attorneys' egos have them over-ride this common sense objective. They want the clients to defer to them for *every* question and action – to be the end all in the transaction.

Everyone has their roles in a transaction, and obviously, values, housing markets, school districts, and other similar matters fall solely within the responsibility of a real estate agent. The attorney has not spent months learning and working within the clients tastes, criteria, and finances. Nor do attorneys stay on top of the market or homebuyer trends. Personally, I would *never* try to answer those questions, as it is obviously the real estate agent's domain to commandeer.

When an attorney throws their weight and opinion into an agent's area of expertise, it can very quickly weaken the relationship between the clients and agent and unravel months of work on the agent's part. I wish to add legal expertise to the transaction, *never* to devalue the agent. On the flip side, the last thing a real estate agent wants to be found guilty of is practicing law without a license! With regard to legal advice and documentation, you and your clients are better served to allow the attorney to assume such risks on their behalf.

• Keeping Clients' Emotions in Check

An attorney works to keep clients' emotions under control throughout the transaction. Although I'm certain it's frustrating and likely insulting to the real estate agent, and comes about many times without justification, it is often the case that during emotionally-charged situations and negotiations, the attorney is the only voice of reason clients will respectfully respond to. In such instances, attorneys should be credited for keeping the *deal alive.*

Transactions can prove to be months-long nightmares for some clients. In my experience, during 99% of every residential transaction a buyer or seller at some point feels like they do not want to go through with the deal. How often have you had to work with:

o A seller offended by a buyer's offer?

o A seller or buyer experiencing remorse?

o A seller frustrated with inspections?

o A buyer that is convinced he's buying a money pit?

o A buyer overwhelmed with lender requests and problems?

These are all factors that push clients into *highly emotional states of mind,* and it is up to the attorney to not only handle the protection methods of ensuring the contract and other documents are adequate as previously discussed, but also keep clients under control so that their decisions are not based on irrational or emotional thoughts.

I remember when I was buying my first house – I told my wife that *we were not closing* if the bass boat in the garage was not included (a bass boat of all things). Fortunately, after intense negotiations, it was included and our transaction closed. That bass boat sat unused in our garage for two years until I had to sell it. (I believe the sales price allowed my wife and me to go out to dinner one night at KFC®. What could be more rational then jeopardizing a home purchase over a Bucket of Extra Crispy and side of slaw?) As my own experience proved, clients lose perspective and need an attorney to either act as a sounding board while they release steam or to make the actual decisions for them, so that their final decisions are, in fact, rational.

Have you had the oh-so-fun experience of sitting at a closing table when the buyers' monies are not in on time? If you have not yet, let me assure you – you will soon. I believe it's a real estate agent's rite of passage. The emotional sellers will start threatening that they intend to keep the buyers' deposit and then sell the property to a third party.

It is very easy for an attorney to step in and recite that the contract does provide those rights and encourage the sellers to be aggressive because that is what the contract says on its face. However, an attorney is also there to advise them of the *resulting practical effect of their decision*:

1. The sellers would have to spend money on having those monies released from escrow.

2. The sellers would have to expect that the buyers will raise an argument, legitimate or not, to tie up the property so that it cannot be sold to someone else.

3. The sellers would have to initially pay attorney fees out-of-pocket, although they may recover them.

I always share with my sellers that even when past clients have won the escrow, the amount of time and money spent almost always forced them to revisit their decision with regret. It is not uncommon in Florida for escrow disputes to take up to a minimum of nine months and incur a minimum of $40,000 in fees.

By educating clients as to the time and money outlay their emotionally charged decision could cost them, an experienced attorney usually diffuses these volatile situations.

Unfortunately, when an attorney is not already involved in such a transaction, a much different ending can result:

1. The well-intentioned real estate agent tries to calm the sellers and explain the likely repercussions.

2. The sellers grow more irate and jump to the concussion that the agent is unconcerned about the sellers' best interest and only wants the deal to close so he/she can get paid the commission.

3. Sellers storm out, ending any chance of a successful closing, with the parting phrase of, "We're calling a lawyer!"

Unfortunately, it is easy for clients to fight when they think their position is supported by the contract and they don't understand the practical and/or economic risks involved. How many sellers would not close the next day if they knew that there was a possibility they could not close for a year? Is that scenario really something worth pursuing? There may be a few sellers who do that, but once most people gather their thoughts and begin to think rationally, they tend to focus on what is in their best interests. Interestingly, it was their best interests that brought them to the closing table in the first place – *they are there to sell their house and a strong attorney will keep their focus on achieving that goal.*

The same principal applies to buyers. How often do agents find themselves trying, albeit often unsuccessfully, to calm down and rationalize with buyers who are extremely upset at sellers for failing to fix a negotiated repair prior to closing? Unfortunately, it seems the closer an issue arises to the closing date, the more suspicious emotionally charged clients become of real estate agent's advice – fearing they no longer are interested in protecting their clients but rather looking out for their commission. In this scenario, once again, the attorney is frequently the preferred voice of reason and will try to have both parties negotiate a solution, for example have the sellers' escrow monies for the repair item or possibly reduce the sale price in a cash deal scenario. If a solution can't be agreed upon, often the attorney has to help keep the dollar amount of the repair in perspective for the buyers. An attorney would explain that it would be irrational for the buyers to risk their escrow monies for a repair that only reflects a negligible percentage of their purchase price; they could end up spending thousands of dollars over a few hundred dollars.

- **Advise On and Resolve Issues**

An attorney is retained to advise on issues and resolve them if they can be resolved. Every closing has an issue of one sort or the other, and sometimes they cannot be resolved. However, having an attorney involved up front helps provide a proactive approach, so if an issue does arise, you will have sufficient time to address it. Also, if problems arise earlier on in a transaction, the clients are always in a less emotional state, and therefore, thinking and acting more rationally.

During the week of closing, when the bank is calling for things and people are yelling about problems and scheduling movers, the clients' emotional levels peak. When an attorney has to be hired in the 23rd hour, everyone's patience is gone – nobody is thinking rationally. Remember what we said above. You may have reached the point of no return with those clients, and they may just give up or feel that they are going to give up. An attorney helps recognize those issues in advance and can explain the problems to clients so that they understand their risks. Viewing it from the agent's perspective, I would think the attorney delivering bad news takes some of the "shoot the messenger" backlash off of you. It is not guaranteed that the clients will not be upset or feel beat down, but having an attorney comfort and explain certain details early in the process helps control the clients' emotions and provide sufficient time to address those issues, rather than ask for an extension on the day of closing. Good attorneys are *proactive*. They do not need someone to bring the problem to their attention – they can *foresee* the problem. A successful attorney endeavors to resolve problems and keep the transaction on track because the main goal is to sell and/or buy – *that* is the reason the contract was signed in the first place.

- **Make Certain Deadlines Are Met**

I create the deadlines based upon the contract. I am the one responsible for making sure your clients meet all deadlines. As a competent real estate agent, you know how crucial it is to stay on top of contractual dates. You are responsible for these deadlines if I am not involved on the transaction. Let me provide peace of mind for you and your clients to ensure that your clients' contractual deadlines are adhered to. I also follow up with all other parties to make certain they meet their deadlines, creating a second layer of protection for your deals, relieving you of unnecessary responsibility and lability.

- **Know How and When It's Time to Apply Pressure**

Lawyers are feared simply for being lawyers. That being said, other lawyers, simply because they too are lawyers, are not fearful of one another. A good lawyer must know when and when not to apply pressure. The end goal is for a transaction to close and protect your clients' rights without allowing egos, attitude, or simply the lawyers themselves to get in the way. Have you ever had a transaction in which someone keeps on taking and taking and taking? An attorney gets involved and all of a sudden the taking stops. Sometimes you have to respond and other times you do not. My rule of thumb on every transaction is to do everything I can for the other party within reason. If they ask for something unreasonable, we attempt to let them know in a delicate manner why we do not think we are responsible or that their request is too broad. No need to argue and no need to talk down to, yell, intimidate, or agitate. Deals are hard enough. This is the time to be friendly and personable and explain why you cannot do something. If the other party keeps on pushing then the friendly approach might have to be reconsidered. Every now and then parties in a transaction need to be *firmly* reminded what they legally can and cannot do.

I once had a client who was buying a house, before my involvement, who was informed by the seller that they no longer intended to sell the house. Rather than calling the seller and sending a demand letter, I reached out to the listing agent, whom I knew, and asked if it was necessary that I file a lawsuit right now or if she could give me adequate assurances that within three days everything would be back on track? The seller was simply being emotional and everything worked out in the end. My client saved thousands of dollars because the seller was responsive. Being an aggressive attorney I could have easily just filed the lawsuit and had the same result, but the costs would have gone up, *and the closing would have been delayed.* A good attorney knows there is a time to apply pressure and a time to be delicate.

- **Help People**

Each of the objectives discussed above directly relate back to the simple premise that an attorney's main purpose must be to ethically represent and help people. An experienced and strong attorney helps their clients and the real estate agent by staying true to their objective of advising their clients of the consequences of their decisions, right or wrong, and letting them know what the future has in store for them.

I enter into every client relationship with good will. I take my responsibilities seriously and work to make certain that every client is better off for having hired me.

CONTRACT PREPARATION

I have encountered and worked through thousands of problems over the years. Based on these experiences I have included central concepts to help you better understand the general risks involved in preparing real estate contracts. Ideally, you will want an attorney to prepare contracts for you; they can assume the risk and better protect your mutual clients. If your clients refuse to hire attorney representation, do pay close attention to the following:

- **Listing the Parties**

One would think listing the parties to be a very simple task. You determine the owner of record and that should be it. However, this is not always the case.

Homestead Protective Rights – In Florida (and possibly other states as well), there are homestead protective rights for the spouse, so you must consider the spouse who is not always listed on the title. Should you include such spouse in the contract or not?

In my 20 years' experience, I have had a few experiences wherein only one spouse signed a contract and thereafter decided they wanted to back out of the transaction (no longer wanted to sell). When buyers in those situations opt for the contract to be specifically performed upon, the seller is then required to convey the property to them. However, since the untitled spouse did not join in (was not named on) the contract, defenses are raised that the contract cannot be specifically enforced because of spousal homestead rights. (The buyers in these situations can still have maintained claims for damages, but often they want the house.) Also, as a reminder, if a contract is specifically enforced and a closing occurs, then naturally a commission is due to the real estate brokers.

The foregoing is an example of the thought process which goes through an attorney's mind when getting involved on a real estate transaction. Attorneys know that what you may have been taught in real estate school, to simply list the owner of record on a contract, is not enough. Do you want to be the agent who did not include the spouse, precluding your buyer's rights of specific performance and limiting their ability to have a deal close? Are you comfortable with not receiving a commission on the transaction, and in addition, subjecting yourself to claims for not representing your clients to the fullest extent? Pass this responsibility on to the lawyer. Not every matter is a strict breach of a fiduciary obligation, but as everyone is aware in this day and age, it is very easy for your clients to file a lawsuit. Therefore, why wouldn't you hire an attorney?

<u>Other Owners of Record</u> – In a situation in which you are representing buyers purchasing as a life estate, probate, or corporation, how should that property be listed? One point to consider is the initial party's assignability (whether your buyers may convey their rights and obligations under the contract to a third party before closing). Many real estate agents have represented clients who attempted to purchase a property when the contract is not assignable, and the sellers become difficult by not allowing your buyers to transfer to an entity, to themselves and/or their spouse. Attorneys figure this type of example into their thought process when preparing a contract, and in turn, there are no limitations or liabilities for you or your client down the road.

- **Personal Property**

States with preprinted purchase contracts frequently include a list of common personal property which conveys with the sale. Have you read the personal property section that is preprinted in the contract lately?

Although most sellers would be willing to sell the items listed (include with the purchase of the home), sometimes sellers direct certain items to be excluded.

As an example, your sellers instruct you in the listing agreement to exclude a chandelier from the sale. However, most of the state based form contracts in Florida (and likely other states) include chandeliers as a light fixture. (As an agent, you should always remind the seller to review this provision to verify exactly which items are to be included and excluded.) First thing I do as an attorney is go over all of these items. Among the duties of a real estate attorney is reviewing all important items of the contract, and personal property is one of them. The attorney can ensure that nothing is signed which contradicts sellers' wishes, thus limiting your liability. If your clients sign a contract with personal property conveying, which the agent was told to have excluded (whether it was in noted on the MLS as excluded or they told you to exclude), then understand that your clients *will rightfully look to you for payment* of such personal property. Do note, writing the exclusion of the item on the MLS listing, while smart practice, does not lighten your liability should the purchase contract fail to reflect it.

Many real estate agents rely heavily upon their memory of outdated forms because they are what they were originally taught on and naturally default to. It is overwhelming keeping up with each new form and contract, but it is important to remember that updates are usually published to address common issues that the earlier contracts failed to address. However, even if you diligently stay on top of changes, you will never be able to acquire the wealth of knowledge attorneys gather through their vast experience with many matters which do not relate to forms.

Attorneys bring both a second knowledge set *and* a second set of eyes. Have you ever read a form so many times that you reached the point where you think, "I simply cannot read it anymore!?" A second set of eyes is needed to catch common oversights. Attorneys are required to read each form each and every time, a practice that protects you and your clients. Perhaps your preprinted contract does not have a washer or dryer listed in the list of items to convey. A practicing and knowledgeable attorney will address this common issue by asking the agent or clients if there is a set in the home that should convey. Do not be the agent that funds a personal property mistake out of your commission.

• Dollar Amounts

The purchase price figure is the one contract component that all buyers and sellers understand, and the real estate agent consistently gets right. However, extended closing dates, changes to figures or financing amounts, and the initialing of changes allow for problematic discrepancies that attorneys are in a unique position to identify and address.

A common financing inconsistency occurs when negotiations find the parties agreeing on a higher purchase price from the buyers' original offer without the original amount to be financed being adjusted accordingly. For example, if the original offer was $100,000 with a mortgage of $80,000 (80% loan to value – LTV), and negotiations end at $115,000 purchase price, but the amount to be financed remains unadjusted at $80,000. The real estate agent, prior to having parties sign, should have adjusted the loan amount higher to $92,000 to keep the 80% LTV in effect. Unfortunately, the buyers have now *unintentionally yet contractually* agreed to complete the transaction as long as they can obtain financing for a mere 69% of the loan. When the property appraises at or above the $115,000, the appraisal contingency will be satisfied and therefore the rights allowed the buyers through the contingency (to rescind the contract or negotiate the purchase price lower) will no longer be an option. The bank will commit to lending the $80,000 as the $115,000 confirms there will be more than enough equity in the home to limit their perceived risk. The financing contingency will have been fulfilled, and as such, cannot be used as an out for the buyers. The end result – the buyers are contractually obligated to bring an additional $12,000 cash to the closing table or be slapped with a failure to perform, resulting in a possible loss of deposit, attorney fees, etc. Guess who is going to be named in a resulting lawsuit? That's right – *the real estate agent* who failed to adjust the amount to be financed accordingly. Once again, an attorney can both protect your clients…and you!

Attorneys are required to read the contract closely, looking in particular at figures to minimize their clients' risk (and what goes hand in hand with this is minimizing *your* risk). More importantly, they protect your clients by ensuring they are only obligated under the contract as *they* expected under the contract. In the example above, your clients were not expecting to come to closing with $35,000, only $23,000 along with 80% LTV financing. The attorney becomes the lead party to catch those discrepancies. What happens if it is missed by the attorney? It now becomes the attorney's problem.

- **Dates**

There are certain nuances in every contract which attorneys are required to be aware of. Deadlines missed by oversight or date overlaps are commonly a problem. In fact, some states' contracts are drafted with the understanding that "time is of the essence," meaning every date is a *hard* date for performance failure. Contractual dates should not be taken lightly.

Attorneys prepare detailed timelines so that their clients are aware of each and every deadline and due date in the contract. They keep timelines consistent because they've seen what can go wrong on a regular basis. You should never miss a deadline due to mere oversight when you could easily have had an attorney review or even prepare the contract for you.

Over the years, I have observed certain deadline issues to be common. For example, Additional Deposits are usually due on or after the last day of the Inspection Period. However, it is common for real estate agents to extend the Inspection Period, but fail to extend the date of delivery of the Additional Deposit. Generally both sides continue on with the contract and the deposit is delivered at the end of the new Inspection Period, with no one making an issue of the discrepancy. However, when the sellers need to delay closing, you better believe the sellers' attorney will raise the default argument that the buyers failed to timely make their Additional Deposit. In essence, they would be forcing the buyers to accept the extension or risk their deposits being kept and losing the home.

In Florida, and perhaps it is true in your state as well, the most common mistakes attorneys see with timelines are associated with the date to cancel due to lack of financing. As of now, buyers who have been denied financing must cancel at least seven days *prior* to closing. I cannot tell you how many real estate agents miss that deadline as opposed to attorneys, who are all too aware of its importance. Also, when extending a financing commitment deadline as the closing date nears, sometimes it extends within this seven day period, creating an overlap. It is imperative to have an attorney involved so that these discrepancies do not occur.

- **Time**

Is time of the essence or is it not? In certain states like New York, generally transactions do not involve time sensitive closings wherein time is of the essence. Certain buyers or sellers do not even realize "time is of the essence contracts," such as those standardly used in Florida, have an absolute deadline for closing. Always look at your contracts to see if time is of the essence to ensure that the deadlines will be followed.

Another common oversight in contracts is whether or not the contract involves business days or calendar days. Always make sure that you review the contract form and any changes to verify whether calendar days or business days will be employed. You do not want your clients thinking they are selling their property 45 days from contract signing when in fact it is 45 *business days* from signing.

Certain time deadlines should always be addressed jointly in a contract. Generally, in an "As-Is" contract (wherein buyers has an absolute right to cancel), you never should have an Additional Deposit (or a second deposit) due before the expiration of that Inspection Period. For this reason, I generally make the delivery of an Additional Deposit no earlier than one day after the expiration of the Inspection Period. Why would you have your buyer put up the balance of their deposit (10% or other amount) when they have not made a determination if they are proceeding forward with the contract or not? Although those monies are refundable, there are certain sellers that wish to give buyers a hard time, and therefore do not release their monies from escrow. As opposed to having $10,000 held up, your buyer might have $150,000 if they are required to advance those monies before the end of the

Inspection Period. Do not ever allow your buyer to be required to make that deposit before the end of the Inspection Period. Fortunately, most agents are aware of this when they initially prepare the contract, but when changes start to go back and forth they forget to make those changes.

When you change the Inspection Period, remember that you need to change the time period for the deposit if it is based on number of days. If it was based on the Inspection Period, then naturally, you would not need to make that additional change. For example, you start out with a 25-day Inspection Period and 25-day deposit period and the sellers counter with a 10-day Inspection Period and 10-day deposit period. You quickly counter with a 15-day Inspection Period, forgetting to change the Additional Deposit. The buyers are now required to deposit the monies by the tenth day. If they do not make timely deposit, short of cancelling prior to that time, (which we do not want to be in a position to require), then your buyers will be in default. *Whenever changing the Inspection Period always change the date of delivery of the Additional Deposit.* As a final reminder, when extending the Inspection Period, always remember to include an extension such as, "The Inspection Period <u>and time for delivery of the Additional Deposit</u> is extended to…" Problem solved. On the positive side, even if you do miss that deadline, generally things will work themselves out. However, over my years I have seen it all, and I recall a few instances where sellers needed additional time to move into their newly constructed house. They subsequently requested an extension from the buyers and the buyers refused to extend because they had every intention of closing on time. The first question from the attorney was, "Did the buyers perform, starting with deposits?" Turns out there were changes made to extend the Inspection Period but not the time for delivery of the Additional Deposit, and therefore, the deposit was not made timely. Now the sellers had leverage on the buyers – right or wrong, the buyers are not in an absolute positon of compliance whereby they have 100% satisfied their obligations under the contract. Do not forget to whom the buyers will look to blame when that situation arises. Why not get an experienced attorney to alleviate those issues and your responsibility?

There are usually two types of contracts that can be employed – one being an "As-Is" Contract and the other being, what I refer to as, the "Standard Form" of Contract.

The As-Is Contract allows buyers to generally cancel within the Inspection Period for any reason whatsoever. This right to cancel is not as favorable to sellers because buyers can walk for any reason whatsoever, even the most ridiculous determinations. Buyers have the sole discretion to cancel. However, the sellers in these situations, to their favor, have no obligation to repair or replace any items identified by the buyers.

As to the "Standard Form" of Contract, sellers are generally obligated to repair structural items up to a certain amount of monies once identified by the buyers. It is favorable to buyers, as items identified during the Inspection Period are contractually obligated to be repaired by the sellers. It is negative for the buyers, because sometimes the sellers may meet those contractual obligations, but they do not meet the standards that buyers are looking for. These "Standard Form" Contracts are favorable to sellers because, unlike an As-Is Contract, buyers become "locked in" to the contract without the absolute ability to cancel. However, it can be detrimental to sellers since they now become contractually obligated to spend monies to do repairs.

In my experience, I prefer when an As-Is Contract is employed. During the Inspection Period the buyers can cancel for any or no reason whatsoever. Even though this provides a "mirage" whereby buyers can depart from the contract, I find that during the initial 7-10 days from the Effective Date is when buyers are most likely to determine that the repair items scare them, or they are not willing to undertake that type of work. In essence, if they make that determination, it is usually best to move on rather than deal with the legal battle that might ensue later. (Lawyers often get involved to explore those options.)

Oftentimes during the "As-Is" Inspection Period, there may be items that are brought to all parties' attention, and this provides opportunities to negotiate. Sometimes sellers might say it was "As-Is" and they are not required to perform repairs, but, for example, a common buyers' response is that they did not contemplate putting on an entirely new roof. In such an event, hopefully a contract can get resurrected and/or those items are repaired. If that was a "Standard Form" of Contract, you might have a dispute wherein the sellers state they will *repair* the roof, but the buyers obviously requests full roof *replacement*. In this scenario, nobody would close, thus wasting 45-60 days and upsetting your clients, whose anger will often be misdirected at you. On top of it, a lawsuit might ensue.

Keep in mind, the Mold Inspection Addendum provides a type of "As-Is" cancellation due to mold, so if this is included in the "Standard Form" of Contract, you may want to consider simply employing the As-Is Contract because using the Mold As-Is creates an absolute right for buyers to cancel, so you might as well apply that to all inspections and not just mold. (The "Standard form" of Contract in Florida does not address mold.)

Most contracts have a specific deadline when a contract must be cancelled should a buyer not obtain a loan commitment. For instance, the most recent versions of form contracts I have reviewed have a seven-day limit prior to closing. As an agent, you must always make a note of that deadline. You must always make sure there is no overlap between those two dates. For instance, if you have 45 days to obtain the loan commitment, you should make sure that your right of cancellation of seven days falls *outside* of those 45 days. To be clear, if you sign a contract on January 1st and your loan commitment deadline is February 15th, you always want to make sure that the closing date is *at least* seven days beyond such date so you can properly cancel the contract, if need be, without the buyers jeopardizing their deposits and potentially being forced to perform.

What would happen if there was an overlap? I do not know, but let's avoid that. For example you have 45 days from January 1st, but your closing date is February 15th. When can the buyers cancel the contract, if the dates indicate possibly after closing? There is no definite answer, but other than improperly preparing a contract, why would we put ourselves into that situation? Always make sure that your deadlines do not overlap. Avoid such an overlap by either amending the closing date to give yourself the window (e.g. make it February 22nd) or modify the seven-day period to reflect a shorter period so there is no overlap (e.g. you can now cancel up until two days before closing). This is what attorneys look for, and although annoying and detailed, we are the ones that are presented with the problems on a regular basis due to oversight (often due to lack of experience) and overly anxious parties setting a too fast pace to exercise care. If your buyers cannot obtain their loan in accordance with the contract, they must cancel within that time period or their right to cancel is waived. Simple enough.

- ## Acceptance of a Contract

To have a binding contract you must have an offer and acceptance of the same terms that were previously sent over, and further, delivery of acceptance of the offer. Generally, when the contract comes into effect, that date is determined to be the effective date. As you are delivering the acceptance of the previously sent, unaltered contract, state in the email that, "Today is the Effective Date." This will assist all parties to the transaction, and any attorneys, with constructing the contract timeline. Likewise, if someone sends a contract to you and it is exactly the same as what was sent to them, then you simply respond "Thank you. Accordingly, today is the effective date." The email will serve as record in case there is a dispute.

What happens if you are sent back an offer with three changes and your clients agree to *only* two of them (as evidenced by only initialing next to two), make an additional change regarding the third, and you send it back to the other side? To be clear, you do *not* have an acceptance.

However, if your sellers' agent sends over a contract signed and initialed in its four places by the sellers, and the buyers initial three of the changes, but does not otherwise alter the contract and sends back the same document without changes, then you have a binding contract. I get a lot of dispute on this, but the buyers accepted exactly what was sent over. Think about it – if the buyers did not accept one provision they would have crossed it out before sending it back. In such scenarios, agents often want to get the missing initials. However, doing so could suggest a new effective date has been triggered and therefore the Inspection Period could start later. If you do request that initial, make sure you are just clarifying that it is for your files, and nothing changes the presently executed legally binding contract and effective date of sale.

Keep in mind, on occasion a lender will want you to re-sign a previously accepted contract because it is not clear enough for them to read. How do you prepare that document? Do you simply re-sign the contract with the old date? This is where lawyers get involved. There should be some language referencing the old effective date and other retroactive provision so that you do not extend the Inspection Period. Imagine having all parties sign that contract to appease the lender only to have the buyers cancel the next day, even though the Inspection Period under the original contract expired 15 days earlier. Guess who the sellers will be angry with? Get an attorney involved.

Lastly, I am not a fan of sending over one page at a time during the acceptance phase. I prefer that the contract, when it is signed and exchanged, includes all of the pages. (This might just be the lawyer in me talking).

- **Preprinted Language**

Preprinted language in contracts is a bit like background music. At a certain point you don't hear it anymore. Everyone becomes so accustomed to preprinted language that they often fail to realize when certain situations are missing or when irrelevant matters are included.

Nowadays, many brokerages require their agents to include preprinted language in their contracts. They tell you it is standard and therefore it should be acceptable. Who is it standard for? You need to review the language and make sure that beyond a shadow of a doubt there are no issues with the preprinted language and that it is applicable to your clients' transaction. Just because it is typed does not mean it is acceptable; and by having your clients sign something you could be obligating them to additional issues or concerns, including financial obligations. For example, the preprinted language in the contract reads, "Seller will satisfy any and all liens and assessment on the Property." There was a city municipal lien that was passed which was payable in installments and collected on the regular tax bill (although there was another provision in the contract that addressed this, it was neglected in that section). Because of this overriding language, the buyers insisted that the sellers pay the balance of that lien which was to be paid over a period of 15 years after closing, costing the sellers additional monies to the tune of $35,000. To this day, I believe they are still in litigation trying to settle with the real estate agent. In addition, the preprinted contracts cannot anticipate every single situation and/or issue that arises. For example, in certain standard contracts the buyers are required to obtain their open permit search during the Inspection Period, a practice which rarely occurs. Title companies will order open permit searches, if required by contract or requested by buyers, but the results typically come in *after* the buyer's protected Inspection Period. Consider changing that language up front. Otherwise, your buyers will end up being forced to close with open permits, and they will ask you why they were not protected. Hopefully you did not tell them they did not need an attorney! This is what experienced attorneys do – look for issues in the market and address those up front.

As mentioned earlier, preprinted personal property lists can easily create problematic situations within the contract as well. Never have your clients sign for items that do not exist on the property; always strike through such items. Moreover, never fail to write in items that do convey with the property, should they not appear as one of the preprinted items.

Checking off Boxes – You must always review the boxes that are left blank in any contract.

Closing Disclosures – In some states you are required by law to make certain types of disclosures. Required disclosures sometimes call for *anything* that materially affects the property value. Sometimes disclosures require things that materially affect the value, *which are not readily observable*. Always play it safe. *When in doubt, disclose.*

Property Disclosure Forms – Some states have developed preprinted property disclosure forms for sellers to complete. Agents should recommend sellers write in anything additional that could be construed as possibly having a material effect on the property. With such disclosures, at least the sellers have disclosed the items on the form to the buyers. Should the sellers leave out something that should have been disclosed or fail to answer a question accurately, this could give rise to an accusation of fraud. If such property disclosures are not required by law in your state, you will have to weigh whether disclosing on such preprinted forms is best.

Mold – Be careful with preprinted mold inspection addendum. In Florida, and perhaps in your state, preprinted addendum for mold inspections are often attached to the standard contract, as the matter is not covered within. The addendum allows the buyers to cancel without penalty if mold is found with a remediation cost above a predetermined dollar amount. Essentially, such an addendum turns a standard contract into an "As-Is" contract, and therefore the sellers must be notified to the created contingency. It is for this reason that I oftentimes convert the entire contract into an "As-Is" contract because, in essence, the buyers already have the right of cancellation in their mold inspection provision.

Condominium and Homeowners' Disclosures – Always remember to include these legally required disclosures. If you fail to do so and the buyer party has a right to cancel, your sellers will blame you. On a side note, you must read these preprinted forms because incredulously enough, they expand certain obligations of parties therein. For instance, the condominium rider in Florida contains a provision that a seller has obligations to pay for any special assessments which were discussed during the minutes of the condominium board meetings over the prior 12 months, if they did not disclose those to the buyer. How many sellers have you represented that have attended every one of those meetings? In essence, as lawyers, we review these provisions, are familiar with them, and we change them. Do you want to be the same real estate agent that is getting sued because he had his sellers sign the preprinted form? Do you want to hear your sellers say to you, "How would I know that? I never went to any meetings. Why would you let me sign that?" That is what lawyers are here to do.

Occupancy Agreements – There is a preprinted form that addresses this type of situation. Have you read that closely? If the actual lease or occupancy document is not agreed upon than either party at a later date, either party may cancel the contract. Is this what you really want? Or do you want the parties locked into a deal?

Sometimes you are not aware of this situation upfront when the contract is signed, and you later learn the buyers need to move in before closing or the sellers need to remain in the property after closing. Obviously nobody likes this situation, but sometimes it is a necessity.

Why be the one preparing pre- or post-occupancy agreements and assume all the liability attached to it? This is just one more example of why you would benefit from your clients hiring an attorney.

UNAUTHORIZED PRACTICE OF LAW

In the end, the unauthorized practice of law is growing, and so is its enforcement. Clients will try to have you take on unnecessary risks by working outside the boundaries of your real estate license just so they can avoid paying an attorney fee. You do not want to be the subject of an investigation pertaining to the unauthorized practice of law. Find an attorney to help you on the contract, provide you guidance throughout the transaction, and relieve you of responsibilities and liability. You aside, it is also in your clients' best interest to have an attorney represent them.

I do not understand all the nuances of a house, let alone have a firm grasp on the market place, and as such, I would not try and broker a transaction. I do not act as a real estate agent now, nor will I ever try to. *I would be doing a disservice to my clients by attempting to provide services outside of my scope of knowledge.*

Always work within your knowledge base, and leave law to the attorneys…

TITLE INSURANCE

What is title insurance? Unlike casualty and liability insurance, which protect you from incidents that occur in the future, title insurance protects you against incidents or occurrences *that happened in the past.* Title insurance is, in essence, the guaranty that when you acquire real property, the only items or matters (oftentimes referred to as encumbrances) that affect such property are those matters listed in the title commitment, and more importantly, prior mortgages, liens, and other monies due and owing from the sellers or prior parties who owned the property, have been satisfied in full.

When buying a piece of real property – how do you know that you are the person that owns it? How do you know that there are no liens on the property? How do you know that there are no tenants? In effect, you can't simply stand on the property and make the claim that you possess it, therefore you own it. Just because you are standing there does not mean that the mortgages of record go away.

Title insurance provides peace of mind for the new owner. A title company runs searches to make sure that when you deliver your proceeds (and/or the bank delivers their proceeds) at a closing, there have been sufficient monies provided to satisfy any of those monetary encumbrances on the real property. In addition, title insurance also confirms that any parties who own an interest in the real property convey their rights to you, so you own 100% of the real property. Last, title insurance will also ensure/insure that nobody else, (e.g. a tenant), has a right to occupy the real property. After closing, if a seller's mortgage is determined to exist, or someone else claims ownership of the real property (two common examples of potential title problems), it is not your responsibility financially and you would turn over that matter to the title company to address on your behalf (this is referred to as a *title claim*).

As a lawyer, obtaining title insurance is the most important component on any property transaction for my buyers. In fact, when clients suggest they do not want to obtain title insurance, I reply I would have to charge them far more for my time to prepare a disclosure document explaining how *ridiculously stupid the idea of forgoing title insurance is*, than it would cost them to obtain the actual title insurance. Moreover, I highly doubt any disclosure could work in that situation, because it is such a bad decision.

A Look Behind the Scenes at a Title Company

A contract gets signed, inspections are completed, and then the contract gets forwarded to the title company. First, the title company runs a search of the public records to see what affects the real property. Naturally, there may be homeowners' restrictions and general utility easements that affect the real property, which are generally acceptable because, really, there is not much you can do about them.

What are the main issues that are discovered in a title search and need to be addressed by sellers at or before closing?

Mortgages and Liens – If your sellers obtained a loan to buy the real property and/or subsequent equity line, a mortgage should have been recorded. When the search is performed and a loan has been found, it will be identified in the title commitment as a *requirement to be satisfied*. Requirements are those matters which must be satisfied by closing so the buyers will then own the real property free and clear of those monetary encumbrances.

Notices of Commencement – When contractors perform work, they often record notices in the Public Records to ensure that they can get paid for their work, and if not, they have lien rights. If a notice of commencement appears, it will be up to the title company, through work with the sellers and the contractor, to prepare documentation and collect necessary monies so that such notice is terminated. This action further confirms that the buyers will not be responsible for any construction-related liens of the sellers.

Legal Discrepancies – Sometimes a deed is not prepared correctly. For example, the marital status is not listed or there is a legal description discrepancy. Imagine if your buyers believed they were buying a two acre parcel, but the legal description only included one half of that parcel. They would not be very happy when they tried to build! The title company will address those legal discrepancies so that they own the entire property which was contemplated. In this situation, the sellers' title claim would prompt the title company to try to resolve such discrepancies so that the sellers would own what was insured in their title policy. Such actions could include corrective deeds and/or paying monies to third parties to acquire the missing parcel. If they could not acquire the missing parcel through such actions, a monetary payment under the policy would be paid to the sellers.

Probate Matters – If someone dies, there are certain requirements to take their ownership and place it into an estate so that a party can sell. A title company will ascertain if the property has been properly probated with duly appointed individuals to act on behalf of the estate, and if not, a lawyer may be necessary to address those matters.

Homeowners' Dues – Title companies will obtain necessary paperwork to confirm there are no past due homeowners' dues owed by the sellers, and if there are, they will be collected at the closing.

Code Enforcement Liens – There may be a violation item recorded for the property by the local municipality. This must be addressed in two ways. First, the lien amount must be paid off (whether in full or through an approved reduction), and second, the municipality should sign off that the violation has been corrected and satisfied.

After the title commitment is received, the title company will request the paperwork or documentation from the lenders and/or contractors and/or homeowners' association, as applicable to address any of the matters above.

The primary documents requested are those pertaining to the mortgages to have satisfied and a letter from the homeowners association, referred to as estoppel letters. In effect, the title company requests the bank(s) and homeowners' association to state what is owed. The title company will then include those amounts on the closing statement to be collected, making certain they are disbursed to the correct parties thus satisfying those obligations.

In addition to the estoppels requested, generally the title company will request a lien search from the respective municipality to verify there are no hidden monies due and owing from the sellers, such as unpaid water bills, septic bills, or any other bills for services that a municipality provides. If there are monies that are owed, the title company will collect those amounts, or at least they should, to satisfy those obligations.

The title company will typically order a survey to verify that the location of the house and/or additional structures are within the boundary lines of the property. A survey is generally required on every loan transaction. It is strongly suggested for cash deals. A survey is not required for condominiums, but it is required on townhomes acquired through financing.

On any loan transaction, remember that the lender will also want title insurance guarantying that their loan is in a *first lien position*. In addressing the requirements above to provide a title insurance policy to the owner, the title company will also have the same general requirements for the benefit of the lender. The only additional requirements will include the recording of the mortgage and other documentation to lien the property. The title company completes its duties by:

- In a cash transaction, closing the transaction and recording the documents, including the deed, to delete the requirements in the title commitment.

- In a financed transaction, same as above but in coordination with the lender and including their documents.

- At the closing, the title company will run an updated review of the public records and obtain appropriate documents to address the "gap" period. As you will recall, the prior review may have occurred three weeks earlier. So, in effect, the title company is just checking to make sure that nothing has happened within the last three weeks. The issue, though, is that the record search is not usually up-to-date because the property records are a few weeks behind, and therefore, although you might be closing on the 30th, the record search might only be valid through the 15th of the month. Accordingly, certain affidavits are obtained from the sellers guarantying that they have not done anything within that "gap" period. Naturally, if the sellers did and they lied, then there would be a problem with respect to the real property, but based on the title company obtaining those affidavits, that risk now shifts to the title company. (This is the essence of title insurance. The title company assumes the buyers' risk.)

- The title company will coordinate the release of the claims, the handling of the conveyance and loan documents, after obtaining them as set forth above in form and content acceptable to the title company. Once they receive them, along with the monies, they are in a position to record the deed and mortgage and, in effect, assert that the buyers own the real property free of sellers' liens and claims. Such mortgage will now be in a *first* position. In connection with this, although the prior mortgages are still of record, the title company will then disburse the monies that were requested on the estoppel letter to those mortgage companies in accordance with the closing statement (or Closing Disclosure, i.e. CD or HUD), and pursuant to various state laws, those mortgage companies have a certain limited period of time to then record a document called a satisfaction. This satisfaction removes the mortgage from the records.

RESIDENTIAL MORTGAGES

Dear Real Estate Agent,

Having originated mortgage loans for 20 plus years, I truly believe I have worked with every type of real estate agent out there. I have observed, time and time again, what separates *top producers* from the rest of the agents – *they refuse to let anyone waste their time!*

Being in sales, I understand how exciting it is to get a call from new prospective clients. I know you want to immediately dive in and get started showing properties. Unfortunately, this is the worst thing you can do. Whether you are meeting with clients face-to-face or over the phone, your initial contact should be treated as a fact-finding mission. You will determine the type, size, and location of the home your clients desire. Once you know what they are looking for, your follow up question *must* always be, "When we find your next home, how do you intend to pay for it?" If the answer is they will need to finance or mortgage any or all of it, without question you must *insist* they get pre-approved for a mortgage...before visiting homes.

When it comes to mortgages, agents often tell me, "I am not comfortable getting involved or asking my clients about their personal financials..."

Not comfortable???

How comfortable are you spending weeks or even months finding clients a property and getting it under contract only to later find out they can't get approved for a mortgage?

You are better than that. Do not allow your time to be wasted.

Your job is not only to find your clients a home but to guide them through the entire home buying process. You are their trusted advisor. Without question, financing consistently ranks as one of the most confusing and intimidating aspects of the process for buyers. Learn about financing and seek out strong loan officers to recommend – your clients deserve only the best.

Warm Regards,

Gerald Pumphrey

Sr. Mortgage Advisor
Waterstone Mortgage Corporation

THE HOME LOAN

For the average American, a home will be *the most expensive purchase* they will ever make and the *largest debt they will likely ever carry* in their lifetime. Moreover, choosing the right mortgage and working through the process can be an overwhelming experience. Thus, it is *imperative* as a real estate agent that you assist your clients in choosing the right lender to finance their home.

When it comes to financing a home, your clients will quickly realize there is no shortage of mortgage companies to choose from. While all lend money and offer similar products, there are some distinct differences between them.

The first important decision your clients will make is what type of lender they will choose to work with. Today, there are three main types of mortgage lenders:

1. **Banks and financial institutions,** such as Wells Fargo, Bank of America, and Chase, *issue mortgages directly* to individual consumers. They tend to lend their own money.

   The *advantage* is that they handle the five major phases of the loan process internally: origination, processing, underwriting, closing, and funding (each phase to be discussed in more detail later).

   The main *disadvantage* of this type of lender is they are limited to their own products and pricing.

2. **Brokers** on the other hand *act as agents who do not lend their own money*, yet *work with multiple lenders* to find the one that offers the *best rate and terms*. When the loan is taken out, your clients are borrowing from the lender, not the broker who has acted as an agent on behalf of the borrower.

   The obvious *advantage* is that the broker takes the burden of shopping for the product with the best rates and terms off your clients. Brokers, due to their experience with multiple lenders' products, are also in a better position to educate you, the agent, and your

126

clients, as to what is currently available in the market and how one product in comparison with another might best suit a given situation.

The main *disadvantage* of this type of lender is that they do not have control of the entire process. Most brokers handle just the origination and processing of the loan. However, since they do not lend their own money, they do not control the function of underwriting, closing, and funding of the loan.

3. **Correspondent lenders** are mortgage lenders that originate and fund home loans in their own name, which means they *are a hybrid of banks and brokers.* Shortly after the loan closes, they sell these loans to the secondary market. Correspondents fund their own loans and typically handle all five phases of the loan process. Similar to a broker, they represent many lenders, meaning they too offer a wide array of products and pricing. Based on my experiences, I believe correspondent lenders provide the best of both worlds for your clients.

SCREENING LOAN OFFICERS

Your clients will be looking to you for loan officer recommendations. At minimum, check that they are licensed and have no complaints filed against them on the National Mortgage Licensing System® under the consumer access search. Look for reviews online, and make certain either you or another real estate agent who you trust has had a successful closing with them.

As you meet loan officers, always question if you would feel good recommending them to your clients:

- First and foremost, do I like this person? People choose to work with people they like. Remember the typical mortgage closing takes between 30-60 days. Is this someone you can see yourself talking with on a daily basis?

- Are they knowledgeable? They may have an amazing personality, but do they know what they are doing? The answer to this question does not always reveal itself until you have worked with them through a difficult deal or two. It is not always about years of experience. I have worked with some 30-year veterans that are nothing short of tired old dogs. The mortgage industry is constantly evolving. Things are not done the same as they were five or even two years ago.

- Do they work like you? When you refer someone, they are, in a sense, an extension of you. How they perform is a direct reflection on you. You are always available (i.e. evenings and weekends). Do they work the same or are they only available during business hours on business days?

- What is their response time? How long do they take to return phone calls and emails? What do they think is acceptable... two hours or 24 hours? Make sure you are clear with your expectations and they are willing and able to meet them.

- What is their bedside manner? I know it sounds cliché, but I view the role of the loan officer as that of a financial doctor. Too often, purchasing a home is an emotional rollercoaster for our clients. The strong loan officer not only knows their products but also how to keep your clients calm when they get emotional!

Have a sheet with three lenders at the ready for your buyer consultations. It can be presented with a quick, "Since I understand you will be looking to finance a portion of your purchase, please contact one of our recommended loan officers. It is imperative that you start the pre-approval process immediately. As you probably realize, sellers are directed by their agents to not even consider an offer from a buyer that is contingent on financing without a pre-approval letter."

Always have your buyers pre-approved *prior* to showing them property!!! Your time is money. In fact, *there is no better way* to determine how serious buyers are than by letting them know they need to be pre-approved by a lender before you will begin showing them homes. If they balk at the idea or act "offended," they never had any intention of purchasing a home. They did, however, plan to string you along and let you play

HGTV host to their idea of a few fun months of looking at dream homes that they could never afford. They do not respect you as a professional; do not give them your time. Suggest where they can find local open houses advertised and move on to finding true clients. Moreover, should you be approached by owners wanting to sell their home so they can purchase a new one, make certain they get pre-approved for the new home prior to listing their current home for sale. If not, you set yourself up to spend time and money marketing their home for sale that they may later refuse to sell once they learn they do not qualify to purchase a new home in the price point they had expected. Your time is money – always protect it by getting your clients pre-approved!

Once your clients have chosen the loan officer they wish to work with, the next step is to have them pre-approved.

Please understand, pre-qualification is one of the *grayest* areas of mortgage lending. The reason is simple. The definition of what constitutes a "pre-approved buyer" varies greatly from loan officer to loan officer. As such, whenever you are presented with a pre-approval letter from a lender for which you are unfamiliar, I cannot emphasize enough how important it is that you personally pick up the phone and call the loan officer to ask the following questions:

- Did the loan officer *only* speak with the borrowers on the telephone?

- Did the borrowers complete a loan application?

- Did the loan officer pull the borrowers' credit reports?

- Was the borrowers' loan run through an automated underwriting engine to generate a loan approval?

- Did the loan officer review the borrowers' tax returns?

- Were the borrowers' assets verified?

You should *never* just accept a pre-approval letter and assume the loan officer did their job.

This is best illustrated by a real life example. A few months back, I received a call from Rick, who was a past client of mine. He wanted to call to let me know that I would be receiving a call from his friend Betty. He let me know that Betty was in the process of selling her home and would need a mortgage to purchase her next property. A few weeks later, I received a call from Betty and learned the following:

Betty had just received an offer from a buyer wanting to purchase her condominium unit for $225,000 for which she only owed $125,000. She hoped that after paying real estate commissions and closing costs she would net around $85,000.

She was looking to purchase a single family home around $325,000 and wanted to borrow $250,000. She intended on using the $85,000 from the sale of her condominium to cover the down payment and closing costs on her new home.

Betty has been a self-employed hairdresser for the past five years.

At the end of our conversation, I let her know that in order to pre-approve her, I would need her to complete an online application so that I could pull her credit. In addition, I would also need her last two years tax returns so that I could determine her income for underwriting purposes. After receiving her loan application, I proceeded to pull credit. Betty had an 805 credit score and only carried one small credit card balance outside of the mortgage she had on her condo, which would be paid off upon sale. Can't get much better than that!

Even better, Betty listed her income on the application as $5,000 a month. With that income, she would have no problem whatsoever qualifying for a $250,000 mortgage. It wasn't until I reviewed the provided tax returns that I saw we had a problem, *A Big Problem*. The income Betty had listed on her application was actually the gross sales of her hairdressing business. The tax returns showed that the business had monthly expenses of $2,500. This meant that Betty's income for qualification purposes was actually $2,500 not $5,000 per month. What is worse is that with only $2,500 a month, Betty no longer qualified for the $250,000 mortgage she wanted!!!

Now it was time to bite the bullet. *No* loan officer *ever* likes to call a borrower to let them know they do not qualify for the loan they want. In my conversation with Betty, I let her know that she did not qualify for what she wanted. However, she did qualify for a $150,000 mortgage. Unfortunately, this meant that she would have to look for homes in the $225,000 range. Betty was obviously very upset as she was now under contract to sell her existing home. It was scheduled to close in 45 days, and she just now learned that she could not qualify for the price of the home she had wanted to buy. Wouldn't it have been nice if the agent that listed her home recommended she get pre-approved for a mortgage at the time of the listing appointment vs. once she had it under contract??? She was going to start looking at lower priced homes, and she would get back to me once she found something.

Fast forward a week. I get a call from Rick. He just wanted to let me know that Betty had spoken to another lender after we last spoke and that lender told her she could be approved for the $250k mortgage she wanted. Rick could not understand how it was possible that the other lender could approve his friend for so much more than I could. The answer is: they can't! I assured Rick that the other loan officer was mistaken and to please have Betty call the loan officer and to have them review the tax returns again.

Well that was the last I heard until three weeks later when I received a call from Betty. She was in tears calling me to let me know she was a week away from closing on both homes and just received a call from the other lender that the underwriter had declined her loan as her income to debt ratios were too high. You may be saying this could never happen. Well it does – all the time! *A pre-approval is only as good as the loan officer issuing the letter.*

Okay, enough with the horror stories. Let's assume your clients have a viable pre-approval letter and you have now found them the home of their dreams. They have made an offer to the sellers, and the sellers have accepted. It is now time for them to make mortgage application.

PROCESS AND KEY PLAYERS

As a real estate agent, you do not need to be a mortgage expert, but you should at least understand the process and know who the key players are. The mortgage process is broken out into three main stages – *application, processing, and closing.* During each of these stages, your client will be introduced to three pivotal players – *originator, processor, and underwriter.*

1. Application Stage

Once your clients have chosen a lender, their next step is to apply for the loan. Typical purchase agreements call for borrowers to make loan application within X number of days (five is the default in Florida) of executing, but what does that really mean? It is at this stage your clients will be introduced to the first player in the mortgage process, the loan officer also referred to as the originator. The originator works for the lender or broker and will be your clients' main point of contact throughout the entire mortgage process. The originator has several responsibilities:

- Consult with borrowers in order to understand their financial need and goals.

- Explain the various financing options.

- Assist the borrowers in determining which financing option best suits their needs and goals.

- Aid borrowers in completing the loan application.

- Evaluate the loan application and ensure it is complete and accurate.

- Verify the borrowers' creditworthiness.

- Communicate with processor, underwriter, and closer throughout the entire loan process.

It is worth noting that almost every lender uses the same **Uniform Residential Loan Application** or, as it is commonly referred to in the industry as, the **1003**. This application contains 10 sections:

Section I: Type of Mortgage and Terms of Loan

This section details the type of mortgage for which the borrowers are applying. There are five loan choices in the section: FHA, VA, Conventional, USDA/Rural Housing, or Other. Here, the terms of the loan applied for are detailed: loan amount, interest rate, loan term, and amortization type.

Section II: Property Information and Purpose of the Loan

This section lists the address of the property being financed, number of units, year built, and other details with regards to purpose of the loan.

Section III: Borrower Information

This is where the borrower's and co-borrower's (if applicable) personal information will appear. It contains borrower(s) social security number, date of birth, marital status, and contact information (last two years residency addresses and telephone number).

Section IV and V: Employment Information and Monthly Income and Combined Housing Expense Information

These sections will list the name, address, and telephone number of employers for at least the most recent two-year period. This section details the break out of the borrower's monthly income. It has separate sections for base, overtime and commission, and other income. This section will also detail how much the borrower currently pays for housing expenses in addition to listing the break out principal, interest, tax, and insurance (PITI) payment that will be on this new loan.

Section VI: Assets and Liabilities

This section lists all bank accounts, savings, retirement, and investment accounts. It also lists current liabilities. All monthly debts are detailed based on monthly payment and total balance outstanding.

Section VII: Details of the Transaction

This section details the purchase price of the property, closing costs, prepaid account information for real estate tax, and insurance on loans which will contain monthly escrow, seller credits, down payments, and total cash to close.

Section VIII: Declarations

In this section, a borrower and co-borrower will be asked if there are any outstanding judgments against them and/or if, in the past seven years, they have been foreclosed upon or have given a lender a deed in lieu of foreclosure, or declared bankruptcy. Moreover, in order to learn if the borrowers can qualify for and repay the loan, they must answer additional questions including, but not limited to, if they are:

- Being sued;

- Obligated to pay a loan that resulted in foreclosure, deed in lieu of foreclosure, or a judgment;

- Presently delinquent on any loan;

- Obligated to pay alimony, child support, or separate maintenance;

- Borrowing any part of the down payment;

- A co-maker or endorser on a note;

- Intending to occupy the property as a primary residence.

If borrowers answer yes to any of the above questions, additional paperwork will need to be gathered and reviewed by the loan officer. In addition, it is within this section that a borrower must affirm whether they are a U.S. Citizen or resident alien.

Section IX: Acknowledgement and Agreement

This is the signature section of the application. By signing, one is attesting that the information contained in the application is accurate and true to the best of their knowledge.

Section X: Information for Government Monitoring Purposes

This section contains ethnic origin and race. This is the section the government uses to compile their statistics to ensure the housing finance system is meeting the needs of every racial and ethnic group in the country.

2. Documentation Stage

Now that your clients have completed the application, the loan moves to the document stage. The documentation stage is without question the MOST important stage of the process. It is at this point the originator will review the information provided on the loan application and pull the borrowers' credit.

After careful review of the credit, income, and assets information stated on the loan application, the originator determines if the borrowers qualify for the loan for which they have applied. More often than not, this is accomplished by the originator's utilization of an automated underwriting engine.

It is important to note that the vast majority of mortgage loans today will ultimately be sold to one of the two federal government secured entities (GSE's): Fannie Mae and Freddie Mac. Both Fannie Mae and Freddie Mac provide automated underwriting engines to lenders as a means to help determine whether the GSE's would inevitably purchase the loan from the lender after the loan has closed. Fannie Mae calls its automated underwriting engine Desktop Underwriter (DU) and Freddie Mac calls its Loan Prospector (LP). It is *very* important to note that not all loans are eligible to be run through automated underwriting engines and *approval through an automated underwriting engine cannot be construed as a loan commitment or approval.* Automated Underwriting engines are merely a credit assessment and risk tool used by lenders to determine a loan's strengths and weaknesses. *Ultimate loan approval lies with the underwriter.* Automated approval engines not only determine loan eligibility, but they also let a lender know what financial information will need to be obtained and verified in order to make the loan saleable to the GSE's. It cannot be emphasized enough that these engines are only as good as the accuracy of the information plugged in. The age old saying "garbage in – garbage out" certainly applies here. Below is a generic list of what type of documentation your clients will be asked to provide their lender during the processing stage. This is by no means the complete list, as every loan request is unique. Required documentation includes:

- Year-to-Date pay stubs covering the most recent 30 days;

- Last two years *complete* personal tax returns with corresponding W-2s, 1099s, and K-1s;

- Last two years *complete* corporate returns (for any and all entities which appear on the borrower's personal tax return for which they have more than 25% ownership);

- Year-to-Date profit and loss/balance sheet (for self-employed borrowers, this will again be required for any and all entities for which the borrower has more than 25% ownership);

- Most recent two *complete* monthly bank statements showing where the down payment monies will come from and to document reserves (cash the borrowers will have on hand after closing);

- Copy of drivers' licenses;

- Copy of mortgage statements, insurance declarations page, and real estate tax bill for any currently owned residential properties.

The reason this stage is without question the most important in the mortgage process is because a lender cannot issue a commitment to lend *until they have received and verified all the required documentation*. So many times I hear borrowers say things like:

- "I shouldn't have to provide all this documentation as you can clearly see I can pay for this property in cash."

- "I have an 800 credit score, isn't that enough?"

The truth is NO... NONE OF THOSE ARGUMENTS MATTER! Since the mortgage meltdown of 2008, *all loans require full documentation*. No documentation, limited documentation, stated income loans, etc. are no longer commonly available products.

Once the majority of the documentation and automated approval are received, the originator turns the file over to the processor. The processor is the person that typically handles all the behind-the-scenes items such as ordering the appraisal, title, verifications of deposit and employment, verifying borrowers' social security numbers, and ordering income tax transcripts from the internal revenue service. The processor works with the originator and your clients to ensure that any missing documentation is obtained. The processor's goal is simple. They want to ensure that they have all required documentation in the loan file to ensure that, once it is sent off to underwriting, the underwriter has enough information to approve the loan.

I stated earlier the primary person that has the ability to approve the loan is the underwriter. An underwriter is an employee or representative of the lender. The lender publishes guidelines for which borrowers must meet in order to qualify for a loan. It is the underwriter's job to ensure that borrowers *meet all of these requirements* prior to their signing off on the loan.

3. Closing Stage

Borrowers' typically start to relax during the closing stage. While borrowers might occasionally be asked to provide a last minute item or two, they feel relief that the bulk of document submission is over.

The phrase "the file is now in closing" means that the borrowers' loan file has turned over from the underwriter to the closer. A closer has two primary functions:

1. To work with the title company or attorney handling the closing with balancing the various proration's between buyers nd sellers. The end result determines the final dollar amount the buyers will be required to wire for closing. Due to fraud, most closing agents now require funds be wired (electronically transferred from the buyers' bank account directly to theirs); cashier's checks are no longer generally accepted to fund closings. The title company will provide the buyers with final dollar amount and wiring instructions. Wire instructions contain the title company's or attorney's American Bankers Association (ABA) routing number, which is assigned to each individual bank, and the actual account number it is to be deposited into. Most often, buyers' banks will require they personally deliver the instructions and sign for the wire prior to it being sent.

2. Provide the correct and final closing documents which the buyers will be required to execute at closing.

The majority of the time the closing stage is a relatively seamless process *unless* the amount required to close ends up being very different from the amount the buyers expected. This scenario would likely trigger additional documentation being required from the buyers in the closing stage. More often than not a simultaneous closing, when buyers are selling their existing home and then proceeding to close on their new home immediately thereafter, is the cause of final dollar amounts being off. The lenders have to estimate, to the best of their knowledge, how much the buyers will net from their sale. They will require a copy of the closing disclosure on that home *prior* to releasing docs on the new loan to ensure the buyers have enough funds to close on the new home. It is important in these instances to advise your buyers to let the lender know if there are any material changes to the contract on the home they are selling, regardless if you are representing them on their home sale or not. An example of a jeopardized simultaneous closing follows:

The loan officer estimates your clients will net $10,000 from the sale of their home, of which they will need $9,000 to close on their new purchase. During the process of the sale on their existing home, your clients agreed to a $2,000 credit to the buyers of their existing home as a result of a problematic home inspection. This changes their net to $8,000. They are closing on the sale of their existing home at 9 a.m. and intend on closing on their new home at noon. Their first closing is over at 10 a.m., and they email a copy of the closing disclosure to their lender which shows the $8,000 net for which they actually needed $9,000. They are now $1,000 short of cash required to close! The scramble begins. They now must provide documentation as to where they will be getting the required $1,000 needed for closing. Their file is required to be returned to the underwriter, delaying the closing at best a few hours, or worse days.

PRODUCTS

While you will never overstep your boundaries by advising your clients as to which product they should select, you must have a working understanding as to any product their loan officer puts them with so you can effectively draft their purchase contract.

There are many types of mortgage options available, although the majority will fall into four main categories:

1. Conforming Loans

Too many agents believe conventional and conforming loans are one in the same. Conventional mortgages are loans neither made nor guaranteed by the U.S. government. A conventional loan becomes a conforming loan because it "conforms" to the guidelines set forth by Fannie Mae and Freddie Mac and therefore becomes eligible for purchase by either. While Fannie Mae and Freddie Mac are the two largest purchasers of conventional loans, it is important to note that they *do not* insure these loans like FHA and VA. For this reason, lenders are free to place restrictions commonly referred to as overlays on these loans. Despite these overlays, most conforming loans have the following common characteristics:

- Available up to the current conforming loan limit of $417,000 for single family homes. Loan limit is higher for two to four unit dwellings;

- Require a minimum credit score of 620;

- Typically allow debt to income ratios up to 45%;

- Offer both fixed (10-30 year terms) and adjustable rate terms;

- Up to 97% LTV;

- Typically require private mortgage insurance for any loan to value greater than 80%. No upfront premiums are required and the mortgage insurance automatically cancels once the loan to value reaches 78%;

- Allow sellers to credit buyers up to 3% of purchase price towards buyers' closing costs on loan to values greater than 90% and 6% on loan to values less than 90%. *Credit cannot exceed actual costs.* For this reason, when writing an addendum it is wise to put in verbiage like, "Sellers credit buyers up to 3% of the purchase price towards allowable buyers' closing costs and prepaids." Adding the prepaid language allows the sellers' credit to be used towards prepaid items (first year of homeowners insurance, escrow for real estate tax and homeowners insurance, and prepaid interest) in addition to closing costs.

- Interest rates and monthly private mortgage insurance rates are determined by risk grade pricing. Higher loan to values and lower credit scores will be charged higher rates.

2. Jumbo Loans

A jumbo loan is required when buyers need to borrow more than the conforming loan limit to complete their purchase. These loans, due to their size, are not eligible for sale to Fannie Mae or Freddie Mac. Lenders can either choose to fund these loans with their own portfolio of funds or choose to sell them on the secondary market to investors other than the GSE's. Because these loans have less investors and carry more risk due to their size, most jumbo loans have the following criteria:

- Require higher credit scores, typically 700 or higher;

- Require larger down payments, usually 20-30%;

- Require higher reserves (cash left after closing to cover un-expected/emergency expenses).

3. FHA Loans

An FHA loan is a loan that is insured by the Federal Housing Administration. The program was created back in the 1930s due to the many foreclosures and defaults that resulted from the stock market crash of 1929. The program was originally created by the government as a means to stimulate the economy and housing market. By insuring loans, they incentivized banks to once again lend to borrowers with a lower down payment and less-than-stellar credit. The concept is simple. An FHA loan basically provides the bank with insurance in the event of borrower default. For example, if a borrower on an FHA loan defaults and the total loss was a $100,000, the bank would only lose $70,000 as the FHA insurance would pay the bank the first $30,000 of the loss.

FHA loans have long been thought of as loans for first-time homebuyers. Today FHA loans are popular for many borrowers, first time and experienced home buyers. They allow a borrower to put as little as 3.5% down. This down payment can come from their own funds, a gift from a family member, or some combination of the two. FHA also allows sellers to pay up to 6% towards buyers closing costs and prepaid items. Examples of allowable sellers' contributions include:

- First year homeowners insurance premium
- Prepaid interest
- Escrow set up for real estate tax
- Escrow set up for homeowners insurance

In essence, all of this means buyers can purchase a property with no money of their own. Yet, for the privilege of using the program, FHA charges borrowers an up-front fee of 1.75% (often referred to as a funding fee or mortgage insurance premium). This premium is allowed to be financed into the loan, which is why many FHA loans actually close at a 98.25% loan to value even though the borrowers are truly putting 3.5% down. Here is an example of how it works:

$100,000	purchase price
$3,500	down payment
$96,500	base loan amount
$1,750	funding fee/Mortgage insurance premium
$98,250	max allowable FHA loan amount

In addition to this up-front fee, FHA also charges borrowers monthly mortgage insurance premium (currently 0.85% annually of the loan amount) as part of the borrowers' PITI (principal, interest, tax, and insurance) payment to the bank. It should be noted that FHA loans are now very different from other loans with respect to mortgage insurance. FHA loans originated after June 3rd of 2013, *no longer have the mortgage insurance cancelled once the loan hits 78%*. These loans will now carry mortgage insurance for the *entire term*.

FHA loans do have condition requirements, although they are not as stringent as many agents believe. Agents beware, the FHA is a stickler when it comes to peeling paint on homes built prior to 1978, due to the inherent risk of lead based paint. In addition, on pool homes, FHA requires the appraisers to determine that all pool equipment is in working order and meets local ordinances. In instances where an appraiser is unwilling or unable to determine such, it may be necessary to have a licensed pool company certify that all is in working order.

It is important to note that FHA loans are not an option for every borrower or property for the following two key reasons:

- Each county has maximum base FHA loan limits. You will need to know the limits in the counties for which you work. There are many instances where the county loan limit will be too low for an FHA loan to make sense. For example, in Palm Beach County, the FHA loan limit is $345,000. If a borrower is attempting to purchase a $450,000 home in this county they would have to put down $105,000 in order to secure an FHA loan. Since the down payment in this example is more than 20%, a borrower would most likely be better off with a conventional loan that would not require private mortgage insurance on any loan to value greater than 80%. At times, simply moving the home search over a county line can create more opportunity for your FHA approved buyers. Loan limit amounts may change year to year. Typically announced in December, the new loan amounts go into effect on January 1st and will remain in effect until the end of the year.

- Units governed by condominium associations often do not qualify for FHA lending. FHA publishes a list of warrantable (approved) condominiums for which they will insure loans on. If a specific condominium association does not appear on this list, FHA financing will not be allowed. Factors as to why or why not an association may make the approved list will be detailed in the CONDO FINANCING section.

County loan limits, FHA approved condos, and answers to many commonly asked FHA questions can be found on the HUD.GOV website.

4. VA Loans

VA loans are guaranteed by the U.S. Department of Veterans Affairs. Because these loans are federally guaranteed like FHA loans, they have many similarities except for the fact that they are exclusively available to veterans or their surviving spouses. In short, a VA loan is a no-money-down loan program that does *not* require private mortgage insurance. Similar to FHA, VA loans also charge a one-time funding fee. The amount of this fee varies depending on whether it is a first time or subsequent use loan (between 1.25-3.3%). Like FHA, the funding fee for VA loans can also be financed into the loan. Veterans that receive disability payments from the VA, that are considered at least 10% disabled, are exempt from paying this funding fee.

Unlike FHA there is no maximum VA loan limit; however, VA will only guarantee 25% of the loan up to a current amount of $417,000 (this amount can change yearly). As such, most lenders will require a percentage of down payment on any amount borrowed greater than $417,000. Lenders will ask for the veterans Certificate of Eligibility (COE) in order to determine if a veteran is eligible for a VA loan. For the majority of veterans this eligibility will be detailed in VA's DD form 214.

Similar to FHA, VA also has an approved list of condos for which VA financing can be obtained. The list of condos as well as other commonly asked VA questions can be found at www.VA.gov.

CONDO FINANCING

As a result of the mortgage crisis and financial meltdown of 2008, financing condominiums has become more difficult. The reason is simple. Condos were the number one type of property foreclosed upon during the housing collapse. Therefore, condo lending is under more scrutiny than ever before.

It is imperative that as an agent you are able to explain to your clients the difference between condominium ownership as opposed to owning a single family residence or townhome. In a condo, there is shared ownership. Unit owners share usage and maintenance of the facilities, common areas, and the exterior of the building itself. When it comes to condo lending, banks are not only approving the buyer but the condo association itself. FHA, VA, and Fannie Mae (for conforming loans) publish their own approved condo lists. There are many factors which go into determining whether a condo will inevitably be approved but the most common are:

Reserves: Fannie Mae requires 10% of the condo's budget be placed into a reserve account, regardless of the current balance currently held in reserves. If the condo association collects annual dues in the amount of $200,000, they need to direct $20,000 to their reserve account.

Percentage of Ownership: If 50% or more of the units are investor owned (i.e. not owner occupied), the condo would not meet current approval guidelines.

Insurance: The condo association must have fidelity bond insurance, which protects the unit owners in the event one of the board members steals from the association. Building and ordinance coverage is essential as well.

Pending Litigation: This can kill a deal regardless of who is suing who. Even if the condo association is suing a developer this could make the condo non-warrantable as the lender will be concerned that the developer may counter-sue the condo association in the future.

When it comes to conforming loans, Fannie Mae does not require the banks to delve so deeply into the financials of the condo association when a borrower is putting a larger amount down. They have a "look the other way" approach when their investment (loan) is more secure by a lower LTV. They solely conduct a "limited" review in such instances. In a limited review, the banks are not required to look at a condo's articles of incorporation, by laws, budgets, etc.

A full review is required when a condo is not on an "approved list" and the buyers are looking for maximum financing. The thorough review often finds the condo association's finances do not meet the requirements. If buyers have the ability to put more money down to accomplish a lower LTV, and therefore avoid the full review, it would increase the likelihood of the loan being approved… and you getting to closing.

HOME INSPECTION

Dear Real Estate Agent,

Congratulations on finding a new home for your clients!

I have been contracted by your clients to conduct their home inspection, and I am looking forward to working with you both! Nothing would make me happier than for us to provide a great home inspection experience for our mutual clients.

I deeply believe in the inspection process and the value of the findings report. My home inspection report helps you to help our clients make an informed real estate decision. I am always willing to discuss, in detail, my findings with you both. I will work with you to keep the inspection report in perspective. Sometimes hearing an inspector or their real estate agent say, "Yeah, the air conditioner may be in rough shape, but look at this great roof," or, "Why worry about the cabinets — weren't you planning to replace them anyway?" can put clients at ease.

I have no intention to blow anything out of proportion, or "scare" our clients. At the same time, I will never minimize a potentially serious problem. That would be unethical and a disservice to them. We have the same responsibility and goal — to be honest with and educate our clients. As I tell my clients, we are on the same team: *your* team.

Keep in mind the inspection report is not pass or fail. The results should be interpreted in the clients' interests. A quality inspection report is simply another tool in your toolbox that you can use to help best protect and represent the clients' desires. Take time to review the inspection with your clients. Remember, while you've seen many, this may be the first they have ever read.

As you know, the condition of the property is only one of many considerations when buying or selling a home. Every client prioritizes home criteria differently. Just as you helped your clients weigh other factors — price, location, schools — you can also help them determine how much weight to give to the condition of the property within their decision making process. My company's motto, "*Remember, there are no perfect homes. However, this one may be the perfect home for you!*" speaks to this truth.

See you at the inspection,

Guy Hartman

Owner
Your Inspector Guy

HOME INSPECTIONS FOR THE REAL ESTATE AGENT

Remember, there are no perfect homes.
However, this one may be the perfect home for you!

Over the last few decades home inspections have become an important part of real estate transactions, whether for purchase, sale, or investment. A home inspection provides important information about the condition of a home, which in turn helps the clients make informed real estate decisions. It also helps the clients' agent in meeting the clients' desires and requirements. Perhaps you are working with first-time home buyers. Maybe they don't have the resources to cover immediate repairs or deal with the consequences of a poorly done flipped home (we all know what looks good may not be good). Even the savvy, experienced buyers may be over-awed by the shiny new appliances and do not take into consideration the 15-year-old air conditioner. Nobody wants to face the unhappy buyers that bought a home because of the shiny new granite counter tops and then face trying to sleep in a 90 degree home soon after closing. Your clients need your help in cutting through their emotions and making sure they know what they're getting into.

The purpose of a home inspection is to provide information about the general condition of a property *at the time of the inspection* – a single point in time. The home inspection provision of the purchase contract should be made use of to the clients' full advantage. Even if clients are licensed general contractors by trade, an agent should *firmly push* for a home inspection to be conducted. During the Inspection Period you will want to make certain a licensed professional home inspector is contracted to walk the roof, crawl the attic, examine the electric and plumbing system, and observe the many other items that a thorough, professional inspection will cover.

The clients who ordered the home inspection, and you as their real estate agent, will know a lot more about the property after the inspection. The more you know about the home inspection process, how to interpret the results, and how to prioritize and balance the condition of the property with all the other factors involved in the real estate contract, the better off both you and your clients will be.

The goal of a home inspection is to present the general condition of the property by a third party in an unemotional, unbiased report. The home inspector should conduct the inspection and present the report as an arm's length business relationship. In other words, the home inspector must let the condition of the property *speak for itself.*

Home inspectors do not (or should not) "pass or fail" a property. It is the clients who ultimately make the decision to proceed or not with the purchase, based on how much weight they decide to give to the home inspection findings. Home inspectors *do not* "kill the deal" as some ill-informed agents like to say. Multiple factors are involved in a real estate transaction, of which a home inspection is only one. An engaged, knowledgeable real estate agent helps clients weigh *all* the factors to their clients' mutual benefit. If all the factors are reasonably considered and the client decides to move on to another property – then that is the best course of action for all concerned. Experienced agents know that respecting clients' wishes and helping them make an informed decision, even if it means helping them walk away from a property due to condition concerns, forges a deeper and trusting client/agent relationship, which almost always results in a successful home purchase in the very near future.

WHAT IS A HOME INSPECTION?

As I like to say, *"Roof to foundation and everything in between."* The general home inspection is the most common inspection, but there are many other inspections (discussed later in this chapter). The *general* home inspection is typically the type of inspection addressed in the real estate purchase contract and should be conducted during the Inspection Period if your state contracts offer an Inspection Period. The general home inspection assesses the condition of the subject property *at the time of the inspection.*

Home inspections are often confused with appraisals. Home inspections are about the *condition* of a property and not about the *value* of a property. Once again, the property's condition is only *one* of many factors your buyer or seller will consider in the real estate transaction. As a real estate agent, you will be in a much better positon to advise and help your clients with a solid understanding of the condition of the property.

A home inspection is typically a visual and functional inspection of all the major components and systems in a home – roof to foundation and all the systems in between. Home inspections are not exhaustive and therefore cannot be perfect in spite of the expectation of many real estate agents and clients. However, the good news is that the modern inspection process, executed by a professional inspector, gets very close to perfection. Most deficiencies of consequence will more often than not manifest themselves in some kind of visual indication that the trained inspector can detect and examine further.

Home inspections are solely *visual and functional* inspections:

- If a component can't be *seen*, it cannot be inspected;

- If a component can't be *operated*, it cannot be inspected;

- If it can't be *measured*, it cannot be inspected;

- Latent or hidden defects cannot be reported unless some type of visual evidence exists to indicate their presence.

The inspector will note deficiencies, discrepancies, and/or evidence of the above in the findings report. When necessary, the inspector will recommend certain items receive further review by a specialist. A home inspection can be likened to an EKG your family doctor performs during your annual physical. The doctor examines the EKG results searching for anomalies or indications of problems. If seen, your doctor will advise you to see a specialist for a more in-depth analysis. Home inspections work the same way.

Home inspections are economical in both time and expense. Previously, before the home inspection industry became somewhat established, when one desired to know more about the condition of a home they were forced to contract multiple individual specialists or contractors. For example, an electrician would be contracted to examine the electric system, a plumber for the plumbing system, and so on. Scheduling and compiling the results of the individual inspections was an overwhelming effort on the part of the real estate agent. Home inspection evolved to free the clients and real estate agents from this burden.

Most states require home inspectors to be professionally licensed through the state. In Florida, for example, inspectors are licensed through the Florida Department of Business Profession Regulation (DBPR) just as real estate agents are. For licensure, home inspectors must receive training in the home inspection process, inspection reporting processes, and demonstrate knowledge of all the components and systems in the home.

In addition, most states, including Florida, have established standards of practice that govern the conduct of a professional home inspection. The standards cover what should be inspected, how they should be inspected, and how they should be reported. It is very important that inspectors follow the state standards as they are the legal foundation for the home inspection process.

The condition of the home may not always be determined at first glance and could require further evaluation by a specialist. For example, if the air-conditioning system is not performing it may need repair, maintenance, servicing, or replacement, which can only be determined by a qualified air-conditioning specialist. Often, the source of water damage or stains can only be determined by dismantling or destructive analysis which cannot be done during the home inspection process. This is one reason that home inspections should be conducted as early as possible during the Inspection Period, as this allows time to bring in specialists to help resolve issues revealed during the inspection.

To the comfort of the sellers, and often to the frustration of the buyers, a professional inspection is non-destructive and non-invasive and should leave the home exactly as it was before the inspection. When the source of a deficiency cannot be identified, either dismantling or destructive analysis may be required. For example, a bathroom ceiling stain may be the result of a plumbing or roof leak. Opening the ceiling may be the only way to determine the source. In this case, the inspector should identify the stain with recommendations for further action. The inspector cannot determine the source or recommend the type of repair necessary in this situation.

General home inspections cover at least the following categories which are usually mandated, as a minimum, by state statutes under the home inspection standards of practice. Professional inspectors often cover more areas than addressed by the inspection minimum standards, depending on their experience, training, and qualifications. A good home inspection should encompass all the major systems and components of a home, which include, but are not limited to:

- **Structure** – Identification of the basic structure and structural components of the building along with any deficiencies noted. How is the house built? The report should indicate the type of construction and the materials used. For example, is it wood frame? Poured concrete? Concrete block? A combination of many materials? Often real estate listings, and even municipal property records, are incorrect. Structural deficiencies may be identified by cracks, shifting surfaces, material failure, or any number of other indications. A crack in a poured concrete wall has a completely different meaning than a crack in a concrete block wall. It's very important to know the difference. Repairs, preventive maintenance, and upkeep are different according to structure type; it is important that clients understand what they are buying (and important for the agent to know also). The structural portion of the inspection is usually the most time consuming; it requires the inspector's full attention and understanding of building systems. Indications of performance are completely different between structure types. Sometimes identifying structure is difficult and even good home inspectors cannot determine the exact structure type.

- **Roof** – Should be labeled roof *system* as all the components of the roof comprise a roof system that protects the home from the elements and severe weather. There are many different roof structure types, coverings, and style. Flat, Gable, Hip, and Mansard – the list is long. Coverings can range from concrete tiles to shingles, with plastic or rubber membranes – each with specific requirements for installation, maintenance, and performance. Is the supporting structure a truss system or rafter system? Very important building code differences exist between the two. What kind of underlayment is installed? The home inspector must consider all the above in determining the performance of the roof system. The roof should be inspected by walking the roof from above and from within the attic below if at all possible. My policy is to walk the roof unless safety dictates otherwise – in my opinion walking the roof is the only way to fully assess the condition of the roof system.

- **Attic and Crawlspace** – The places no one wants to go, and I admit, neither do I. However, a complete and comprehensive home inspection depends on entering these areas and inspecting them to all four corners. Another reason to hire the licensed professional home inspector as they are qualified and authorized to enter those areas. These places can be dangerous and damage to the property can occur. It's the last place the professional real estate agent wants their clients or clients' contractor to explore as the owner of the property will expect any damage to be repaired. Attic and crawlspace inspections are the only way to fully assess many of the home's structural components. Attics are *the* place to assess roof performance as leaks will first be revealed on the roof underlayment which can usually be inspected from the attic.

- **Basement** – Like attic and crawlspaces, many structural components of the home are exposed and can be visually assessed by the home inspector in the basement. Basements are probably the most likely place to find important building code discrepancies that are safety related. Many home owners remodel their basements without permits. Unfortunately, the results may not meet important building codes that are designed to provide for habitability and safety. No one wants to find out their clients were trapped in a basement during a house fire due to compromised egress – something that is easily determined by a professional home inspector.

- **Exterior Components** – Exterior components include exterior structure, walls, exterior openings including windows and doors, sealants, caulk and paint, and landscape grade should it affect the home's structure. Many exterior components serve very important functions that are not obvious to most home buyers. For example attic ventilation is often provided through soffits vents. Poorly ventilated attics can cause drastically increased cooling costs, provide an environment for organic growth including mold, and even failure of roof system components due to excessive heat or humidity. Your professional home inspector should spend a significant percentage of the inspection time on exterior components.

- **Interior Components** – Interior components include floors, wall, ceilings, doors, windows, electric receptacles and switches, stairs, railings, and many other items. Water stains, water damage, and unusual wear on any surface should be noted. Often this can be associated with a deficiency found in other parts of the house. Attic underlayment stains over a ceiling stain may, often with little doubt, be associated with a roof leak that must be repaired.

- **Electric System** – Identification of the type or types of electric systems installed (of which there are many) and amperage and voltage ratings. Usually the electric box cover is removed for a detailed inspection of the interior. All accessible receptacles, switches, and wiring components should be checked.

   Case Study – Misidentification of Three Phase Electric System

   A listing agent had stated the electric system installed as a "three phase system," which is a specific type of system not typically installed in residential properties. The buyers owned an extensive and expensive collection of wood working equipment that required three phase electric power. The buyers had based his offer to buy on the availability of three phase electric power. The inspection properly identified the electric system as single phase, which meant that none of the heavy wood working equipment would function in the property. Almost all residential properties are single phase systems, as was also true for this home, with three phase systems almost exclusively installed in commercial properties. The offer to buy the home was rescinded by a very unhappy buyer, who had unnecessarily spent time and money pursuing a home that did not meet his criteria. Tip: utility services will charge more for three phase power systems and will be identified on the electric bill. Review the electric bill to determine if a three phase system is installed in a home you are listing.

- **Heating Ventilation and Air Conditioning (HVAC)** – Identification of the types of systems installed along with a functional check of total system performance. The ages of the major components are often determined and compared against industry standards for expected service life. These systems are very often neglected and can be the source of poor indoor air quality, odors, and even mold. Tip: the cleaner and better maintained this system is, the better the home's indoor air quality.

- **Plumbing** – Identification of the types of water supply and drain, waste and vent systems, and pipes installed in the property. A function check of all accessible plumbing fixtures is often performed. Older homes may have plumbing materials installed that that are now known to cause health issues and lower water quality. Some plumbing materials have proven to be susceptible to leaks and should be identified in the home inspection. Polybutylene supply pipes are one example of a product that has not performed well over time and must be identified in the home inspection if observed by the inspector.

- **Interior Spaces** – Walls, ceilings, doors, windows, floor coverings, and many other components. All accessible interior spaces are checked for damage or any evidence of current or past water damage or staining.

- **Fireplace** (solid fuel burning appliance) – Usually checked for basic safety only, a comprehensive operational check cannot be conducted during the home inspection. Many home inspectors completely disclaim fireplaces. Most fireplace and chimney components are not visible, and as such, a performance and safety review by a qualified specialist before use and at least annually thereafter is highly recommended. Fireplaces and chimneys suffer damage and deterioration even when unused. Remember, as your home inspector will remind all involved: a fireplace is a *fire inside your home*. Take it seriously. A neglected fireplace is a dangerous system. Carbon monoxide detectors are a necessity when fireplaces are installed.

Case Study – Fireplace Glass Door Installation.

Fireplace glass doors should be installed in accordance with the manufacture's specifications by qualified professionals only, and then used in strict compliance with their specifications.

Glass doors can interfere with the proper draft of a fireplace and lead to very high temperatures within the firebox.

An owner installed glass door on an existing fireplace. The home was severely fire damaged after the first proudly lit fire. A torch effect developed through the glass door gaps that far exceeded the temperature rating of the metal insert. The home owner learned a very expensive lesson along with some very unpleasant conversations with the local fire marshal. I always alert homeowners of the perils of fireplace glass doors. By the way, if you are dealing with a home that has fire damage, the local fire Marshall may have very useful records of the event.

- **Household Appliances** – Functional checks of all installed appliances should be conducted. All timers, cycles, and features cannot be checked. Of course required utility services must be available. Recommend that any existing registrations, manuals, keys, or codes be transferred to the buyers, especially for new appliances.

Case Study – Flipped Home

Let's face it, there are some very poorly done house flips out there. With the fantastic high definition television these days I can even identify deficiencies in the latest HGTV house flip program just by watching!

Remember the typical flipper is in it for one thing: maximized profit. This is achieved by low material expense, low labor expense, and fast schedules leading to lower carrying costs. One particularly egregious flip company would install a set of high-end appliances during showings and then rotate them to the next flip. They were replaced with a visually similar set of much less quality just prior to closing. I recommend documenting make, model, and serial number for all appliances. Use your cell phone and take a picture if you prefer, it only takes a second. Make sure you and your clients are paying close attention during the final walk-through if you are involved in a flipped home purchase!

- **Performance Indications** – Indications of deficiencies such as settling, current or previous moisture or water damage, previous or ongoing repairs, or anything else that affects the condition of the property should be noted on the findings report. Gas appliances or systems should be checked for gas leaks and proper installation. Systems that are reaching the end of their useful service life should be noted in the finding's report in accordance with the standards of practice.

WHO SHOULD HAVE AND ORDER A HOME INSPECTION?

Who orders a home inspection greatly depends on what purpose the inspection will serve and the type of property. Most home buyers should order a home inspection within the allotted inspection timeframe of the real estate purchase contract. Home sellers, owners, and investors can also greatly benefit from a professionally conducted home inspection.

- **Resale home buyers** typically will benefit from a home inspection and may need your help ordering one. The buyers can use the results of the inspection to factor in the condition of the property, along with other details, in the decision to move forward with the purchase of the property. Moreover, the inspection can help buyers budget for identified repair expenses as well as expected general ownership costs associated with owning the home after purchase. Many buyers also use the inspection report as a foundation for negotiating repairs, although that should not be the sole purpose of the home inspection.

- **New construction buyers** benefit from a home inspection as much, or even more, than buyers of resale property. In fact, a newly built home is the perfect time for a home inspection! Of course, newly constructed homes are inspected by the local building department that issued the required building permits; however, these inspections *are not as detailed* as a comprehensive home inspection. Building department inspections are performed solely in the interest of public safety and welfare. They are based on local and national building standards, building codes, and, often times more problematic, property record verification. As long as the newly constructed home meets the *minimum* standards of the building department, it *must* pass the inspection. Quality or workmanship is usually not a building department inspection criteria or standard. Furthermore, functional checks of installed systems are almost never done by the building inspector and are not conducted by the vendor. Typically, the first time installed systems (appliances, air conditioning, etc.) are operated is during the home inspection. Building code inspections are generally in place to protect the community, not necessarily the individual purchaser.

Case Study – New Construction Inspection

The first areas I inspect during the roof inspection are areas that cannot be seen from the ground. The newly constructed home had been signed off as complete by the builder's quality assurance department (who is usually the site foreman), and approved by the local building department as ready for the real estate closing, title transfer, and allowing occupancy by the new owner. In one case, I discovered a large area of exposed wood underlayment where the roof covering had not been installed! Everyone from the roofer to the foreman had verified the work complete by looking at the roof from the ground. My policy is that when a roof can be safely walked, it should be walked. If it can't be seen, it can't be inspected. Damaged roof components and leaks would have occurred within the year from this mistake and would have resulted in very expensive and invasive repairs. I saved the buyers and the builder from a very costly and time consuming repair situation, as many home inspectors do.

- **Home sellers** do order home inspections, although this is not as common. In fact, home sellers and their real estate agent have much to gain from having an inspection conducted *prior* to showing the property to prospective buyers. A strong agent will recommend one to the seller for the following reasons:

  1. The inspection findings can become a "punch list" of items for the sellers to tackle. This removes the burden from the agent

"guessing" what needs to be done. Sellers can schedule repairs on their own schedule and receive quotes from multiple contractors to get the best price, instead of being part of stressful negotiations within the sometimes short contractual time frames of the real estate transaction.

2. Presenting prospective purchasers a copy of a recent inspection at the time of showing may put them at ease. However, you might consider keeping the inspection report of findings confidential. Regardless of whether the home has been inspected by the sellers, the buyers should have a completely independent inspection done so their interests are fully represented. To the sellers' detriment, the buyers' inspector may tend to be more detailed during their inspection when they know another one exists, as the last thing they want is to "miss" something another inspector caught (we're only human!).

   Remember that a home inspection report should not be used in lieu of a disclosure statement. Items required to be disclosed per real estate law may differ from those items that were reported in the inspection report. Home inspections are conducted to home inspection standards, which may be and are often far different and much more detailed than those required for disclosure. Ideally, sellers should reference items identified within the inspection report that warrant disclosure on their seller's disclosure form.

   Once, or if, repairs are conducted, present a comprehensive package of work orders, invoices, transferrable warranties, and/or guarantees for any items that were repaired recently (or any time).

3. Lawsuits are often filed when buyers believe sellers have knowingly failed to disclose property defects. When was the last time the sellers were in the far corner of the attic where evidence of roof leaks exists? Better to learn now and disclose rather than be accused of hiding a defect later. And agents – let's face it, sometimes your sellers may not be completely forthcoming due to fear of possible costs triggered by disclosure, or may honestly, yet incorrectly, believe something is too minor to bother

disclosing. In both instances, the unbiased, written home inspector's report helps you. *Keeping in mind of course that home inspections are not, however, disclosure statements and cannot be used as such.* Disclosures must still be made through the real estate contract and transaction disclosure process as state or federal regulations may apply. *Many states have specific statutes prohibiting the use of home inspections as disclosure statements.*

Case Study – Seller's Inspection

A home was inspected for a seller that had a recent roof covering replacement a short four years earlier. The roof underlayment inspection conducted from the attic revealed several areas of active water leaks that were certain to be found by the buyer's inspector. A quick phone call to the roofing contractor resulted in repairs being handled under the seller's warranty within the week. The seller built up trust with the eventual buyer by fully disclosing the leaks and repairs, provided repair orders to the buyer, and was able to transfer the roofer's warranty to the new owner. A smooth, stress-free closing resulted. A buyer can't ask for more than that!

- **Investors** can greatly benefit financially by ordering scheduled home inspections. Periodic scheduled inspections protect investments by catching issues *before* they become major expenses. An annual inspection is a great way to take positive action in preserving the condition and value of their real estate assets. Scheduled inspections are far more cost effective than the typical reactionary property management company method of waiting for a problem to arise before taking action as associated rush fees are incurred to maintain functionality for tenants.

Landlords can use home inspections to document the condition of a property before and after a lease. Inspection reports could cleanly support landlords' claims to withhold security deposits, as a judge would likely favor the unbiased report over a landlord said/tenant said scenario. My company offers an additional cost-saving service to landlords, a tenant education program. At the time of the home inspection, we teach tenants basic hands on maintenance functions and provide them with written instructions to reference over the course of their occupancy. No reason the air filters, for example, shouldn't be changed after that! Educated tenants are more likely to identify and therefore report potential issues and stay on top of up-keep items, which save landlords money and time.

- **Current home owners, *even with no intent to sell*,** can benefit from home inspections. Like investors, home owners, can determine and assess the need for routine maintenance and keep tabs on the performance of major systems like the roof covering or electric system. Even home owners who are very good at maintaining their home can use help in attic reviews, keeping check on moisture issues, walking the roof, or crawling the attic. The sooner a deficiency is identified, the easier and cheaper it is to correct.

Case Study – Current Home Owner's Inspection

Concrete or clay tile is a popular roof covering material in southern Florida and many others parts of the country. Contrary to common belief, this type roof covering is not maintenance-free. Seasonal and daily heat-related expansion and contraction will often cause cracks that may lead to structural damage. The tiles are somewhat fragile and suffer damage even if not walked on. Tile roofs (any roof covering for that matter) should be reviewed annually to ensure all tiles, shingles, membranes, and underlayment are in good repair and structurally secure. While damaged tiles may not be a leak issue, as the underlayment provides such protection, they are susceptible to wind storm damage. Once the wind lifts a damaged or weakly attached tile, the damage can zipper up the roof, meaning each subsequent tile lifts off the next. Secure and properly installed tiles can withstand higher wind loads and may prevent roof failure during a hurricane or less severe wind storms. Many tile roof owners are not ready for the next hurricane. An annual checkup by a professional inspector (or licensed roofing contractor) is highly recommended.

- **Renovators and remodelers** that take advantage of a home inspection during or after renovation, additions, upgrading, or major repairs (particularly for older homes) often benefit similar to the new construction inspection case study above. Older home construction may not easily conform to new building codes, materials and installation techniques. Shortcuts are often used that may not be caught by the prime contractor or the building inspector. A comprehensive home inspection, before project completion or even after project completion, can save a renovation from disaster.

TYPES OF HOME INSPECTIONS

There are many types of home inspections that serve a variety of needs. The person ordering the inspection will select the best type for their situation, maybe requiring multiple inspections or a more tailored inspection than the typical general home inspection.

Insurance underwriters often require inspections based on insurance regulation *as opposed to* home inspection standards. They may be, and often are, completely different and serve different purposes than the typical home inspection. For example, insurance policies (and premiums!) depend on the structure of the home, type of installed systems, and equipment and materials used. Insurance companies sometimes utilize home inspectors to verify the above rather than using staff personnel. When conducting insurance inspections, the home inspector is inspecting to an insurance standard *not* a home inspection standard.

Loan officers may need insurance rates to fall below a certain amount in order for loan approval to happen for some buyers. Their clients will be directed to make certain all insurance inspections are done to help ensure the lowest possible insurance premium is obtained. The loan officer may also have requirements set by certain loan programs (government backed FHA or VA loans for example). These requirements are usually integrated within the program's appraisal program, but this is not always the case. The appraisal process in some programs can be similar to home inspections, but they serve different ends – the home inspection is about the *condition* of the property – the appraisal is about the *value* of the property. In general, home inspections are much more detailed. A side note: an identified safety issue can prevent the completion of an appraisal until the item is corrected.

It is important that you, as a real estate agent, find out from all parties which inspections your clients need and double check that the proper inspections are scheduled. Work closely with your clients' insurance agent and mortgage officer to make sure there are no missing requirements that can delay your closing. Avoid the day-before-closing panic phone call asking for an inspection report that wasn't done!

When home inspectors exercise their home inspection license they must abide by governing regulations. However, with the appropriate disclaimers and agreements, the home inspection can be modified to fit almost any situation.

Types of home inspections include but are not limited to:

The General Home Inspection – The general home inspection is an assessment of the general condition of the subject property at the time of the inspection. The general inspection typically covers roof to foundation and all the systems in between. This is, by far, the most common type of inspection, and though called by different names throughout the states, it is customarily the inspection addressed in the real estate purchase contract. The general home inspection is typically the first inspection done during the Inspection Period. The results of the inspection may indicate the need for further review by other specialists. Try to schedule this inspection *as early in the Inspection Period as possible* to afford the most opportunity to effectively manage identified issues.

Other types of inspections may be included, or specifically excluded, from the general home inspection, depending on the applicable state regulations and local real estate market.

Termite Inspection – Termite inspections are usually heavily regulated with specific inspection and reporting requirements independent of home inspection standards. Typically, they are not called "Termite" inspections as the word "termite" implies an identification of a specific organism. In Florida, termite inspections are called Wood Destroying Organism (WDO) inspections and are regulated by the Florida Department of Agriculture. WDO inspections must be conducted by licensed pest control operators, certified and qualified by the department of agriculture.

Case Study – Termite Damage

I consider preventive treatments for termites a mandatory requirement of home ownership responsibilities – especially in tropical environments such as southern Florida. Termite prevention is often neglected, with potentially very serious and expensive consequences. Wood is in every house, even masonry or concrete homes. One of the saddest situations I have experienced was a seller's inspection for an elderly couple who believed they were protected by their concrete block home. The inspection revealed termite related roof structure damage that was not repairable. Most of the roof structure had to be replaced. The repair bill was just shy of $100,000. Protect yourself and your clients! Make sure your home inspector is also looking for termite damage, even in the case of a seller's inspection. Many states and lending institutions establish termite inspection standards as discussed above. As an agent, you do not want to be pursued for not recommending a WDO.

Mold Inspection – This is a very complicated subject. Consumer and real estate professional education and knowledge on this topic is very weak. Objective data is hard to come by, and when it is available, it is difficult to analyze in context of residential property real estate transactions. Decision making is often driven by strong emotions, based on sensational and anecdotal evidence that is wildly out of proportion to reasonable concerns. I believe that much of the mold inspection business industry is based on fear. The consequences of mold, whether real or perceived, can quickly spiral out of control, even when the root issue and resolution is simple.

Regardless, we are all routinely faced with clients who are naturally concerned about mold. If your clients insist on a mold inspection, of course you would never refuse their right to one, but perhaps the thoughts below can help you help them make certain their decision is based on fact rather than emotion. With that, I share some comments and advice, based on my personal experiences as a licensed mold assessor and home inspector. *Disclaimer: these are my opinions only and in no way should be interpreted as advising against a mold inspection.*

- Education and knowledge is paramount. An hour spent reading the latest guidance on the Environmental Protection Agency's (EPA) website will help you and your client. There is good news in the latest guidelines, even the EPA is learning (and admitting) that it's not as bad as we once thought. The correlation between health issues and mold is not cut and dry (no pun intended – however cut and dry may be a good idea...)

- Mold sensitivity is a health issue that should be discussed with medical professionals. Your local home or mold inspector is very, very rarely such a professional. Personal health issues concerning exposure to mold and *many other common household chemicals and products* should be assessed in light of a professional evaluation of the sensitivity. Mold may not be the problem, if there is one. Self-diagnosis of mold sensitivity is never a good idea.

- Mold inspections must follow strict and rigorous industry standards and protocols. An accurate mold inspection depends on proper preparation of the property. *A viable mold inspection should NOT be done during the turmoil of a home inspection – beware of combo home and mold inspections.* Done properly, a mold inspection should be a separate inspection conducted during a dedicated time period when the conditions at the property can be controlled.

- Because of the above, if done properly, a mold inspection can be a fairly expensive proposition. Be very wary of cut rate mold inspections. Buyer beware, you get what you pay for – especially when it comes to mold inspections and home inspections!

- When I have the opportunity to discuss the issue with my clients, I recommend establishing a valid reason to conduct a follow up mold inspection only if the situation warrants. During my general home inspection I look for any indication of mold growth and conditions that might promote its growth (note that mold or mold type cannot be identified or specified within home inspection standards). I will make a recommendation, based on the condition of the property, on whether the expense of a mold inspection may be warranted. I handle the possible presence of mold just like any other system. In the same way roof covering repairs are recommended, a recommendation for follow up on mold inspection by another independent, professional mold inspector or hygienist can be based on actual conditions vs. emotions. If the purchase contract includes a mold inspection addendum with a period that extends five to seven days past the general home Inspection Period, a professional mold inspection can be conducted without having to get an extension signed by all parties.

Mold growth depends on moisture; mold will not grow in the absence of moisture. Stop the moisture, stop the mold. A dry environment is likely a mold-free environment. If you see it or think it – stop the moisture, dry it, clean it, or remove it until any indications of mold no longer exist –all within the EPA guidelines.

There is mold in every house – all one can do is reduce the risk of exposure. Preventive measures are the best defense against mold.

Tips for reducing the risk of mold exposure:

- Immediately fix any water leak regardless of the source. Leak repairs must include complete drying of all affected material. Never enclose wet material. Unventilated wet material *will* support mold growth.

- Properly operating air conditioners are also de-humidifiers. Use them to your advantage to reduce humidity within your home. Large homes may benefit from additional humidity control.

- Air conditioner systems also, however, create a natural environment supportive of mold growth within the internal components that can affect the living space air. Keep them well serviced, clean, and dry. Replace filters regularly. Keep condensate drain systems and overflow pans in good repair and free flowing. Routine professional servicing and cleaning is a sound investment.

- Keep plumbing drains clean and clear.

- Keep toilet rims clean (don't look – just clean) and lids down.

- Indoor plants support an environment conducive to mold growth. Keep the humidity down!

- Stop all instances of standing water in sinks, showers, bathtubs, washing machines etc. Water should completely drain from all plumbing systems.

- Outdoor pets are exposed to mold. Wash before bringing into the home.

- Keep indoor pets clean and groomed.

Case Study – Mold

The new vacation home owners decided to save money by shutting off water and electricity while they were away. As a result, there was no air conditioning during these times away from the property. When they returned, the interior walls were completely covered with mold (or something that looked like the possibility of mold as home inspectors say…). They were predictably very upset and were looking for someone to blame, other than themselves of course. Real estate agents please note they were very upset with their real estate agent because she did not tell them this would happen! I agree with you, a completely groundless complaint, but a testament to the litigious world we live in.

Insurance Inspection – Insurance carriers often require inspections used to assess risk for a particular property. These inspections frequently require the inspector to follow regulations established by the state's insurance regulatory body. For example, in Florida this body is the Florida Office of Insurance Regulation (FOIR). These inspections should not be confused with a general home inspection, as they are conducted to completely different standards and documentation requirements (sometimes insurance inspection standards don't exist). Some insurance inspections are well regulated by the FOIR, others are not. See the four point inspection discussion below. Insurance inspections should be provided to the insurance carrier.

Depending on local or state requirements there could be many types of insurance inspections. For example, California building codes incorporate strict seismic structural requirements that may require validation. Geotechnical inspections conducted by a soil or civil engineer may be required depending on the type of soil or rock strata on which the home rests. Sinkhole inspections are another example, required in many areas in Florida. Areas that are exposed to hurricane force winds often require a structural inspection to assess the susceptibility to destructive wind force. (Florida wind mitigation inspections are discussed below.) Insurance companies may also have their own inspection requirements that vary between carriers. In Florida, a four point inspection is often required for a home over 25 years old. A Florida four point inspection is also discussed below.

Wind Mitigation Inspection – A wind mitigation inspection is used by the insurance company to assess a property's level of protection against destructive wind, or hurricanes in the case of eastern coastal areas. The FOIR requires premium discounts, often significant, based on the wind mitigation inspection findings. Insurance wind mitigation inspections are very misunderstood within the real estate community, and unfortunately for our clients, many insurance brokers themselves do not have a complete understanding of the form. Wind mitigation inspections can significantly reduce the homeowners' policy premium. The premium reduction can make the difference in the affordability of the property and thus, the difference between closing and not closing. The best time to do a wind mitigation inspection is during the home inspection, as it is easily incorporated into the home inspection process.

The wind mitigation consists of seven sections that cover everything from the controlling building code under which the basic structure was built to the type of window and door protective devices installed. The purpose of the inspection is to determine the *weakest* protection level in each of the seven sections. The weakest protection found in each section sets the level for the entire section. For example, a single unprotected window determines the protection level for opening protection (section seven) as "no protection" even if all other windows and doors are protected.

Case Study – Wind Mitigation

It is important to note that destructive wind coverage does not cover water damage caused by flooding, which is, of course, common during a hurricane. Make sure your client has a thorough conversation with their insurance agent to ensure they understand their policy. You want to avoid the angry phone call from the clients after their water damage claim is denied because you said their insurance would cover them against hurricanes.

When listing a home, be careful when describing the hurricane protection level of the home. One of my clients was very upset with both the listing and buyers' agents as the property was described as having "impact rated windows." The client obtained insurance quotes (unofficial of course) based on the description in the listing. The actual quotes were almost double the estimates as the wind mitigation inspection reflected that some of the windows were not protected. The resulting loss of premium credit was very upsetting to the buyer. When listing a home, make sure your description accurately describes the home!

Four Point Inspection – A four point inspection covers four primary components of the home: Roof, Plumbing, Electrical, and Heating Ventilation and Air Conditioning (HVAC). It is a very basic validation of the type of systems and type of materials used, along with a basic functional check of each of the above. The four point inspection is used to assess insurability of the property and may reveal serious issues that prevent binding (issuing) a policy. For example, policies may not be issued when galvanized plumbing pipes are identified. If there are any deficiencies listed on the four point inspection, the policy will typically not be issued until they are corrected. Unlike the highly regulated standardized wind mitigation inspection, four point inspection requirements may vary between insurance companies. Since the inspector does not know which carrier the insurance broker will choose, the inspector may include more information on the four point inspection, which unfortunately may not be advantageous to the clients.

There can be many more insurance inspections or certification requirements, especially for older homes or specialty type properties. Make sure your clients engage in dialogue with their insurance agent to avoid missing inspections that will inevitably become an issue the day before closing.

Case Study – Insurance Inspection Requirement

I find that how a question is asked often determines the answer. An example from my aviation background may help demonstrate. When asking air traffic control to verify an altitude assignment, for example, the question should be open ended – "verify altitude" versus "verify 10,000 feet." The question should not contain a possible answer. We're only human; it's easy to latch onto the easy (possibly wrong) answer – even for professional pilots and air traffic controllers – and insurance agents! In my experience, asking an insurance agent if they need XYZ inspection is almost a guarantee that XYZ will be needed, regardless of the actual requirement. So…using phraseology like, "What inspections do my clients need?" might result in a thoughtfully considered answer and ultimately a smoother closing process.

CHOOSING A HOME INSPECTOR

Choosing a home inspector is not an easy task. There are many factors to consider, some of which are outlined below. Remember, the home inspection process is outlined in the real estate contract. Licensed, qualified professionals are required. Professional referrals based on a professional selection process is in everyone's best interest.

Look for an inspector who can help put the inspection and inspection process in context, who can confidently explain what they are doing, why they are doing it, and how to interpret the results. A confident, professional demeanor is important for you and the clients. Home inspectors work for your clients, so their concerns should be professionally addressed.

What to look for and avoid in home inspectors:

Independence – The inspector must be completely independent with no financial or business relationship with any brokerage, real estate agent, or any other party to the real estate transaction. Be very careful with inspectors that participate in "pay to play" – another name for kickbacks. Some brokers or agents accept a fee for offering home inspector referrals, which is against most state regulations, including Florida. It is not possible to conduct an unbiased inspection when there is any type of collusion, intentional or not, between the inspector and real estate broker or agent. Even the perception of collusion could place the real estate agent at risk if a problem presents itself after closing.

Focus on Home Inspections – The selected inspection company should be focused on conducting independent home inspections. Inspectors offering services based on the results of a home inspection or upselling additional services should be avoided. Some inspection companies are sidelines to other businesses. My company provides home inspection services only; we are not operating other businesses that may affect our complete focus to the client's home inspection.

Current Licensing, Training and Insurance – Anyone conducting home inspections in Florida must be licensed through the Florida Department of Business and Professional Regulation (DBPR), just as real estate agents. Check your state licensing requirements for home inspectors.

Inspector Scheduling – Home inspections require the full attention of the inspector. Companies that over-schedule their inspectors should be avoided.

Understanding of the Real Estate Transaction – An understanding of the home inspection section of common real estate contracts and how the inspection process fits into the sale transaction as a whole is a must.

Rates and Fees – Look for fair rates and fees based on value, quality and industry standards. Rates are not the best way to choose a home inspector. As you know in your line of work, there is always someone that will do lower quality work for less.

Report Quality and Quality Assurance – A report quality assurance program is a must. An inspector reviewing their own work is never a good idea. Reports delivered on site *will* contain errors.

Professional Associations – Look for inspectors with membership in professional associations. Not all associations are the same. Some are marketing oriented and focus on getting business, not necessarily working the business. Look for membership in the American Society of Home Inspectors (ASHI) or an established state association like the Florida Association of Building Inspectors (FABI).

Local and Personalized – A local business that is familiar with your local real estate market, real estate practices, and building construction types is desirable.

Franchises – Some franchise organizations are marketing or business office management systems and may not be oriented toward providing professional home inspection services. Processes, scheduling, services and rates may be based on corporate revenue requirements as opposed to local conditions and client requirements. Research home inspection franchises before recommending.

Contractors – Be careful. Anyone conducting home inspections must be appropriately licensed and qualified. Contractors are good at what they do, and I routinely depend on their knowledge and guidance. However, the good ones will admit that constructing a house is far different than inspecting for performance during a home inspection. If your clients insist on using a contractor, help your clients make sure they are appropriately licensed, qualified, insured, experienced with the home inspection process, have developed inspection procedures, and can produce a written report that meets professional home inspection standards and the real estate contract standards. See the Focus on Home Inspections section.

Client Conducted – We've all experienced the buyers who want to do their own inspection. See the Contractors section as that advice applies here as well. The advantage of a home inspection as an arm's length, unemotional, unbiased evaluation is lost when buyers conduct them on their own. The sellers could easily, with solid foundation, reject all the findings by buyers. Let me put it this way, *even I would not inspect my own home.* As the saying goes, it is a poor doctor who has himself as a patient.

REALTOR® Association – Many REALTOR® associations have vendor lists that may include home inspectors. They are an often over-looked resource.

PREPARING FOR THE HOME INSPECTION

The key to a good home inspection is access. All systems must be accessible, including electric boxes and panels, water heaters, air conditioner systems, attics, crawlspaces, roof, and so on. All utilities must be on. A checklist including access items is provided at the end of my section.

Who Should Attend a Home Inspection?

The smoothest, most efficient inspections are attended by only the persons buying the inspection and their agent. Many questions can be answered and concerns can be freely addressed on site without confidentiality issues, hurt feelings, or sensitivities. A frustration for home inspectors is being expected to answer questions from the seller or listing agent when it may not (usually not) be in our clients' best interest. If possible, sellers should not attend. Emotions run high when cherished properties are inspected.

How to Use a Home Inspection Report.

Hear me out on this. My experience, after conducting thousands of home inspections and observing the associated interactions between parties, has led me to believe the best way to handle the home inspection is to keep the results confidential until the clients and their real estate agent have had the opportunity to thoroughly review and discuss the inspection report between themselves. Only after this private review should any of the inspection results be released to other parties in the real estate transaction – and then, I strongly recommend only results of concern to the client.

Here's why: the clients' interests are best served when repairs, maintenance, and/or servicing are controlled to ensure work is effected by licensed, qualified professionals following proper repair standards, techniques, and quality of material. In this way, repair invoices, warranties, and guarantees for the work done can be transferred to the buyers. I have faced many situations where an otherwise well-meaning owner, on the afternoon of the inspection, climbs on the roof to make repairs called for in the morning inspection. The buyers could, on solid grounds, reject these repairs, and then call me to inspect them (unfortunately as you all well know, usually on the day before closing). It is never a happy situation to report that the repairs were not done to standard, knowing it will derail your closing.

I realize the above is counter to conventional practice. Many inspection reports are immediately handed over to the sellers with a "fix all this" statement attached. However, I find that everyone in the transaction typically fares better if the results are controlled and released in a purposeful manner. If I were a listing agent, I would not want to receive all the information contained in a professional comprehensive home inspection. I would much rather react to the very likely limited concerns of the buyers. Perhaps one of the buyers is an electrician who is planning on handling electrical repairs themselves – in such an instance, electrical issues not brought up by the buyer are not pertinent to the transaction. Home inspection results handled in a deliberate, confidential process can often help keep transactions on track.

Recommended steps for a buyer's agent to use a home inspection report:

1. If possible conduct the inspection without the sellers present. If that is not possible, conduct the inspection in a confidential manner.

2. Ask your clients for permission to receive the report. Once received, schedule a time to discuss the report with the clients.

3. Your inspector should be happy to answer any questions or address any concerns.

4. After understanding your clients concerns, draw up a list of items the clients would like addressed with the sellers. Present only this list to the sellers.

5. Negotiate confidently for repairs if requested by your clients. Get all negotiations in writing. Monitor repair progress, obtain receipts, repair orders, warranties, and guarantees for your client.

6. Relax. You're well on your way to closing.

APPLIANCE AND HOME SYSTEMS SERVICE LIFE

The best way to determine the expected service life of many systems is to determine the manufacturer's warranty or guarantee period. Installation, servicing, maintenance, repair, and use performed in accordance with the manufacturer's specifications will usually lead to reliable performance and the longest service life. Material quality and workmanship are important factors. This information should be used for guidance and planning purposes only.

Expected Service Life

ITEM	RANGE (years)
Ceiling Fan	5 to 10
Dehumidifier	8
Dishwasher	9
Disposal (food waste)	12
Dryer	10 to 15
Exhaust Fans	10
Freezer	10 to 20
Garage Door Openers	10 to 15
Garage Doors	10 to 30
HVAC Air Conditioner (portable/window)	5 to 7
HVAC Air Handler (inside unit)	8 to 15
HVAC Compressor/Condenser (outside unit)	8 to 10 (6 to 8 for roof top installations)
HVAC Heat Pump	10 to 15
HVAC Thermostats	35
Oven – Electric	10 to 15
Oven – Gas	10 to 18
Oven – Microwave	9
Pool Chlorine Generator (salt water)	5
Pool Filter (cartridge)	2
Pool Filter (sand)	5 to 10 (sand must be replaced every 3 years)
Pool Filter Sand Grid (DE)	5
Pool Gas Heater	3 to 5
Pool Heater – Electric Heat Pump	5 to 8

ITEM	RANGE (years)
Pool Pump	5 to 8
Pool Pump Motor	3 to 5
Range – Electric	13 to 15
Range – Gas	15 to 17
Range / Oven Hood	14
Refrigerator	9 to 13
Roof Covering – Metal	20 to 50+
Roof Covering – Modified Bitumen	10
Roof Covering (EPDM ethylene propylene diene monomer) Rubber	10 to 15
Roof Covering BUR (built-up roofing)	5 to 15
Roof Covering Tiles (Clay or Concrete)	25 to 80+
Roof Shingles Asphalt (3-tab)	10 to 12
Roof Shingles Asphalt (architectural)	15 to 20
Roof Shingles Fiberglass	20 to 30
Roof Shingles Wood	15 to 25
Septic Leach Field	25+ (very dependent on soil conditions and use).
Septic Tank	25+
Vacuum System	20+
Washing Machine	5 to 15
Water Heater	6 to 12
Well Pump	15
Well Pump Electric Motor	5 to 10

Inspection Preparation Checklist

- ☐ All parties notified and informed as necessary.
    - o Date and time
    - o Discussed inspection process with the client.
    - o See property and community access notes below
    - o Schedule sufficient time for the inspection

- ☐ Owner, tenants and all occupants notified.
    - o Inspectors not responsible for coordinating inspection activities with tenants, owners, or other occupants

- ☐ Gated community – Condominium access
    - o Inspector's company and name provided to security
    - o Other inspector information (termite inspector) provided to security
    - o Access, parking policies
    - o Community policies for working hours, weekend, and holiday access
    - o Roof top access policies

- ☐ Property access
    - o Lock box codes and location
    - o Alarm codes
    - o Irrigation system controls unlocked
    - o Fences and gates unlocked
    - o Storage areas unlocked
    - o Utility areas unlocked
    - o Roof top access
    - o Electric meter room access

- ☐ Utilities
    - o Water on with all water shutoff valves turned on. Shutoff valves cannot be turned on by the inspector.
    - o Electricity on with all circuit breakers on. Tripped circuit breakers cannot be turned on by the inspector.
    - o Gas utility on with all gas shutoff valves on, pilot lights on, ignition system accessible.

☐ Access at the property
- o Attic access clear with room for ladders as necessary
- o Storage should not block access to any part of the attic
- o Electric panel clear with room to work and to remove front cover
- o Air conditioner systems accessible (air handler and compressor)
- o Condominium roof and electric meter room access
- o Water heater area clear
- o Electric outlets and switches accessible
- o Doors and windows accessible

☐ Pets and animals
- o Inspections cannot be conducted in the presence of aggressive animals.
- o Pets should be controlled or removed from the property during the inspection.
- o Inspectors are not responsible for controlling pets.

INSURANCE

Dear Real Estate Agent,

Allow me to ask one important favor: please do not consider home-owners insurance an "afterthought" in the transaction.

We are both working together to get to the best possible outcome – a closed sale and satisfied clients. One size does not "fit all" when it comes to insuring what is often your clients' most important asset. The bridge from beginning to end can fall apart if the homeowners insurance is not dealt with properly. It should be a seamless process with no surprises popping up at the last minute. Moreover, a good insurance agent will want to keep you, the agent, involved throughout.

While there are many insurance agents who will obtain a quote for your client, care must be taken to make sure the quote has the necessary coverage and meets your individual clients' needs. Just as we would recommend that our clients choose a knowledgeable and diligent real estate agent, I strongly urge agents help their clients be highly selective when choosing a homeowners insurance broker.

Wishing you success,

Mark Shanz
Broker/Owner
Seegott Shanz Insurance

HOMEOWNERS INSURANCE

Homeowners insurance can prove to be a significant factor in the home buying process. Unfortunately, unknowledgeable real estate agents often treat it is an "afterthought" – an insignificant item to check off their list a few days prior to the closing.

There are **many** different factors that go into selecting the correct policy for each client's needs and their property's particulars. Therefore, you should be ready to recommend reputable, local insurance agents that have various insurance products, get quotes for properties they are interested in as early as the pre-offer stage, and maintain a general working knowledge of the common policies in your market.

Not paying close attention to the specifics of the home insurance in your transaction can *kill your deal.*

Choosing an Insurance Agent

Agents are required to be licensed by their State Financial Services Department. Always check that anyone you recommend is properly licensed with your state.

Most insurance agencies have a specialty line of business. Some are more "financial service" companies. They may offer home insurance as a secondary product in addition to life insurance, annuities, etc. Typically, you will want to work with an agent whose agency's primary product is home owner's insurance, as they are likely to be more competent with it.

The location of the agent's agency should be a factor. You would be wise to choose an agent who is familiar with the area that your clients are purchasing their home in. This can prove helpful as they would be familiar with the typical types of homes and risks in the area and know which of their companies' products would best fit.

Some agents may be limited as to how many companies they use to write policies. You'll want to find agents who represent multiple companies (carriers). The advantage here is that if there are any factors that make the home a difficult risk, having a lot of choices will increase the possibility of finding an appropriate match. No matter what product you need, you would always want more, as opposed to less, choices... *Right?*

You'll need to do a bit of homework to make certain you are referring agents who can properly help your clients with what they need, but that's a small price to pay for a smoother closing.

Too Many Policies, which One Fits My Clients?

There are several different types of homeowners insurance policies. The one that your clients will need depends on three main factors:

1. Who will be living in the home?

2. What type of property (single family, condo, townhome)?

3. Will the home be occupied year-round?

Once you, or your clients, have provided the above information to the agent, an appropriate policy type can be selected. The most common homeowners insurance policies are:

HO-3 – This is the most common policy. It is designed to cover the **full-time owner occupied single-family home**. It can also be used for a seasonal residence. *It offers the most comprehensive policy for your clients.* This coverage requires property inspections and underwriting. Coverage includes *almost* any risk you can imagine:

- Fire
- Smoke
- Theft
- Vandalism
- Water or Steam Damage (pipe, **NOT FLOOD**)
- Wind
- Tornados
- Hail
- Damage from weight of snow, ice, or sleet

- Damage from artificially generated power surge
- Hurricane
- Lightening
- Personal Liability

HO-4 – If your clients are tenants (**renters**), this is the policy type that best fits their need. This policy covers *their* personal items and liability as the tenants. Note that it does **NOT** cover the dwelling inside *or* out. It **ONLY** covers the tenants' contents. This is a simple policy to obtain because it does not require any inspections and little underwriting. However, not all carriers offer this type of policy. Again, make sure to use an agent who has a wide arrangement of carriers. The more products an agent can offer your clients, the better.

HO-6 – This policy is designed for the **condominium** or **townhouse buyers**. In most cases, there is a governing association that has purchased a separate insurance policy, referred to as the "master association policy," to cover the buildings and common areas. Therefore, the purpose of the HO-6 policy is *to cover from the "drywall in."*

This includes lighting, fixtures, cabinets, countertops, just to name a few. It also offers coverage for personal property (contents). The third main coverage of an HO6 is personal liability. Protect against the accidents of others!

DP – Dwelling fire policy – If the property is going to be purchased by an investor and occupied by tenants, this is the type of policy the **buyers/owners/landlords** would need. It covers the building (dwelling) from most events, including fire, theft, wind, and liability. This type of policy DOES NOT cover the contents of the tenants (see HO-4). Any real estate agent representing investment purchasers would be prudent to alert their clients as to the benefit of the DP policy and suggest a clause be included in the lease that tenants must purchase and maintain HO-4 insurance during their tenancy.

It will be very important to make certain the insurance agent has matched the correct policy to your clients' needs. Choosing the wrong policy can lead to the client's insurance being dropped and/or unpleasant consequences in the event of a claim.

Binders

If your clients are approved for a mortgage, the lender will require a binder be issued by the agency. A binder is proof of temporary insurance coverage and assures the carrier is ready for when the property is to close, at which time the full insurance policy will be issued. Typically, the agent can issue a binder 30-45 days ahead of the close date. This binder is a preliminary approval based on the information provided to the agent. Normally, there are no changes, even once the property is closed.

There are, however, situations where a binder can be cancelled, so beware. Typical examples include:

- An outdated electric panel
- An old roof in below-average condition
- An un-fenced pool
- A trampoline is present in the yard
- Purchasers own a vicious breed of dog
- Purchasers had a previous bankruptcy
- Purchasers had multiple prior claims on other owned properties

The more the real estate agent shares about the property and purchasers at the time of quoting, the more time all parties involved will have to either get the issues resolved or find a carrier willing to insure the risk. If the agent does their job, most of these issues should and can be addressed well before closing. There should be no surprises!!! If the closing gets delayed, it is possible that the binder will expire. This means that the policy will have to be re-written, and a new binder window begins. While this should not have any effect on the closing (unless there is now a moratorium in place preventing new insurance from being written due to an impending natural event, such as a hurricane), it is more paperwork for the buyers, as the insurance will have to be reissued.

What's the Cost?

There are lots of items that factor into what your clients will pay for homeowners insurance. Keeping these in mind can help prevent you from wasting time showing a property that becomes out of their price range due to insurance costs. While one high risk factor might not be too cost inhibitive, multiple high risk factors on a single property can drive rates up significantly. Just to name a few:

Age of Home – this is probably the number one factor in determining the possible rate or affordability of the home.

New construction or a home built within the last ten years will typically have the best rates. The roof is normally in good condition. It's been built to the most recent building codes. The insurance company views the home as a lower risk and therefor offers a better rate.

A home 10 to 30 years in age would rate a bit higher. Some of the features may be dated (electric panel, roof, etc.).

A home 30 years or older will be a tougher sell to insurance carriers. However, that does not mean it cannot be done. Finding affordable coverage for an older home is one example when having an experienced, local agent that represents multiple carriers will prove crucial.

Location – Where the home is located has a big impact on the insurance prices. Insurance carriers spend a substantial amount of their resources to determine the risk of certain areas. Often carriers assess the risk as too great in an area and decide *not* to offer coverage for it. The remaining few companies that *do* choose to write policies find themselves in a market with limited competition. As a result, premiums run higher. There is simply too little competition to force rates down (Economics 101). Locations often deemed high risk by carriers that will result in low competition and thus high premiums include:

> **Coastal Property** – The market for windstorm (hurricane) coverage will be limited.

> **Property Without Fire Services** – If the property is located five or more miles from a fire station, or does not have a fire hydrant or viable water source within 1,000 feet, many carriers, due to the higher risk for fire damage, will not offer coverage.

Earthquake Prone Area

Sink Hole Prone Area

Flood/Mud Slide Prone Area

Insurance companies narrow down their rates based on zip codes and counties. So check with your agent if you anticipate any issues.

Construction Type – What material the home is constructed out of is a main rating factor. Common construction types are:

- Concrete Block Stucco (CBS)
- Brick
- Wood frame

Ordinarily, as the fire risk is lower, a CBS home will have a better rate than a wood frame home. However, if insuring in an earthquake prone area, a wood frame home might be considered the lower risk, as its materials allow for a bit of movement unlike a CBS home.

If your client falls in love with a quaint old frame home, located miles from the coast, expect all three factors to be reflected in their insurance premium!

Prior Losses/Claims – Another one of the main rating factors that homeowners insurance companies use is prior claims history. *This is not necessarily exclusive to the property they are looking to purchase.* If your clients have had past claims on other properties, they can expect that to reflect on their insurance quotes. In the case of an "act of God" claim, such as a storm or weather event, most carriers will not hold this against the homeowners. In the event of a water pipe burst, a fire, or a liability claim, this can have a big impact on rates. Carriers believe homeowners who have put through claims in the past are more likely to put through claims in the future, and thus are riskier. Past claims may increase premium quotes, or in some cases, may even disqualify some carriers from offering a quote altogether.

Type of Policy Ownership/Occupancy – Who takes title to the deed and who resides in the property are both factors.

In most cases, the buyer will be purchasing the home insurance in their name or with a spouse/relative. They, more than likely, will be living in the home as a full-time residence. Carriers believe owners are more vested in the property and therefore more likely to pay for timely repairs and maintenance. In such situations, a typical HO3 policy can be shopped around to various carriers for the best price.

If a property is being purchased as an investment, or a corporation is purchasing the property and the residents will not be the owners, rates will increase. The reason that this situation has an effect on the rate is because it changes the type of policy that is offered. As mentioned previously, if the home is not owner occupied, it is written as a Dwelling/Fire policy (DP). In some cases, these rates can be higher simply because the insurance carriers see more risk when the owners are not living in the home full time. Carriers know a vacant home is more likely to experience theft, vandalism, frozen pipes, etc.

Another item that can affect the policy is if the home will be owned by an LLC or Corporation. A large percentage of carriers will exclude liability coverage from the policy in this type of ownership due to underwriting guidelines that exclude this coverage. This is most likely when property is not owned personally, due to the complex possibilities of liability when it comes to LLCs, Partnerships, and Corporations owning property. Discussions would need to take place with the owners and agent to come up with another carrier to write personal liability coverage.

Liability is an important coverage that your client, whether owning personally or through an entity, will not want to go without.

Type of Property – The type of property being purchased changes how much coverage is needed, and thus the cost of said coverage. Homes typically fall under the category of:

- Single Family Home
- Townhouse

- Condo Unit (Co-Op included)
- Mobile Home
- Multi-Unit Residential Building

As mentioned previously, the most common type of policy is the HO-3, which is used for owner occupied single family homes. Since this is the most common purchase and what most carriers compete for, the HO-3 is easy to shop rates for quotes.

If your clients are purchasing a condo/townhouse unit, the type of policy will be different, which will affect the rates. As discussed earlier, most of the time the governing association maintains a policy that covers common grounds of the development and the exterior of the building. The existence of the association's master policy should be confirmed with an association representative when your buyers are contemplating placing an offer on a property. Condo and townhouse owners usually only need the HO-6 to insure the interior of their unit, which is a lower premium than the HO-3 simply because less coverage is offered. I have overheard real estate agents tell their clients that insurance is cheaper when purchasing a townhome or condo rather than a single family home. While that is true in one regard, they should be properly informed that a portion of what they pay in required association fees is to offset their portion of the association's master policy.

Coverage – Coverage can be based on replacement cost value as is true for the HO-3 policy. This means that the insurance company will calculate what the home should cost to rebuild if it were damaged. A number of factors will be used to determine the dwelling coverage limit, including many of the factors above. Once this amount is calculated, the premium can be determined. Obviously, if the home is large or it is an older built home, the premium rates are going to be high.

How to Get the Rate Lower

As any good real estate agent knows, if the prospective buyers cannot afford the home, the deal will not get done! Since homeowners insurance is a key factor in the cost of the home, there may come the time when additional steps will be needed to get a rate lowered to a price that will work for all parties. An insurance agent worth his or her salt will do everything they can to get the best possible rate without sacrificing necessary coverage. Sometimes in markets with little or no competition, we find the "rate is the rate" on the base coverage, yet it is still possible to look at other options which can possibly lower the premium. Every insurance carrier offers premium discounts, and it's up to the agent and buyers to make sure they have exhausted all options. Options to explore:

Adjusting Coverage – Regarding the HO-3 policy, there are six basic coverage items, of which the first three can be explored to possibly reduce the insurance premium.

1. **Dwelling** –The rate is determined based on the replacement cost of the home. In other words, replacement cost is what it would cost to rebuild a home with the same quality and materials on the existing lot. In some areas, replacement cost can actually be *higher* than market value due to the rebuild having to meet the new building codes and accommodate rising material and construction prices. The insurance agent should make sure that the dwelling replacement cost is calculated correctly. If the home is "over-insured" then lowering the coverage can lower the premium without harm to the buyer.

2. **Other Structures** – Other structures refer to unattached items on the property. Sheds, greenhouses, detached garages, swimming pools, driveways, and fences are examples of items considered "other structures" by carriers. Sometimes home purchasers are not interested in insuring the other structures or the home does not have any of these types of structures. Some carriers will do away with other structure coverage all together. Others will require only the minimum amount of such coverage to be purchased. Either situation could result in savings for the buyers.

3. **Personal Property** – Personal property coverage typically includes furniture, appliances, and clothing. Personal property is typically covered at replacement cost. This means that if a claim is filed, it is paid to replace the items at full value. This coverage comes at a high price and can be reduced if the prospective buyer opts to receive actual cash value (ACV) for the home's contents.

4. **Loss of Use** – Loss of use covers additional expenses incurred to keep the homeowners' current standard of living while the home is undergoing repairs due to a claim. The limit is usually set at a default amount and changing it does not affect the premium.

5. **Personal Liability** – This policy covers liability that the owners or family are personally responsible for. The limit is usually set at a default amount and changing it does not affect the premium.

6. **Medical Payments** – Medical liability coverage is for situations in which owners or family are responsible for, such as someone being injured on the property. The limit is usually set at a default amount and changing it does not affect the premium.

Deductible Change – The policy contains a deductible that must be met before a claim is paid. The most common deductible for all claims, not including windstorm, is $1,000. Many insurance carriers offer a higher option of $2,500 or $5,000. Increasing this out of pocket cost can be a nice savings on the premium, in some cases 10% or more.

Alarm Systems – Because the policy covers damage and loss from theft and fire, the insurance carriers offer a discount for having a monitored alarm system in the home. The key word is "monitored." Homeowners will often say, "My house is wired for an alarm system. Why am I not getting a credit?" Carriers know the system does no good if it's not connected and active. The premium credit for the system does not typically outweigh the cost, but it can add up over time.

Credit Rating – Today, a lot of insurance carriers are looking closely at credit scores. We have come out of an unprecedented financially difficult time and many prospective buyers have "black marks" on their credit. In most cases, this will not prevent them from getting homeowners insurance, but their rates may be higher. If your clients have come through the hard times unmarked, they may benefit from a discount. They may even wish to pull their own credit so they know what to expect.

Optional Coverage – The HO-3 policy can sometimes be offered with extra coverage (endorsements) that may or may not be necessary to buyers. For example, there is coverage for screen enclosures or carports that may not be necessary. Removing unnecessary coverage can offer a nice premium savings.

Wind Mitigation – In high risk coastal areas, the wind mitigation discounts can have a *major* impact on the premium. These discounts are given by the carriers based on how sound the home is at preventing damage due to a wind event. The two main areas of concern are the roof and the openings (windows/doors). The carriers use a uniform inspection report, completed by a licensed inspector or contractor, to determine how much of a premium credit is offered to the home. Because the insurance premium can be affected **by almost 50%**, it is in the best interest of the buyers to obtain a windstorm inspection.

Miscellaneous credits – Not every carrier offers the same credits, so it is always a good idea to use a qualified, licensed insurance agent to help navigate through the choices. Some examples of other credits include:

- Senior discounts
- Non-smoker discount
- New wiring in the home
- New construction
- Home being within a gated/guarded community
- Home being within a homeowner association

Talk to your agent about any and every possible way to get the best possible coverage at the lowest possible rate.

Claims and the Closing

The purpose of homeowners insurance is to offer the owners protection against loss or damage to their home or property. It is designed to make the owners "whole" by putting the dwelling back to the condition it was before the event. However, is it wise for owners to file a claim for each and every issue that happens? Not always.

The homeowners insurance policy typically includes a deductible, similar to health or auto insurance. That amount can range anywhere from $500 to $5,000, with $1,000 being the most common. Let's use a small water pipe leak as an example. While the damage is more than likely a covered issue, it may make sense to repair the damage out of pocket rather than file a claim for only $75.

While a claim will usually result in raising the premium at renewal, a claim will also follow the owner's person and can make it more of a challenge to find homeowners insurance coverage in a future home. Insurance companies typically limit the number of claims a person can have before they become ineligible for coverage, and this number is not limited to the home that was involved in the claim. The claim history can follow the sellers to another house they intend to buy. More importantly, *pay attention now real estate agent,* the claim will also remain with the home, making it difficult for sellers to find future buyers as the insurance premium for the property will reflect the claim(s) and will be costlier to insure than other homes in the area.

You may have just found your clients their dream home, but will they be able to obtain insurance? Past claims hovering over a home is not something you will be able to identify when showing a home. What if the previous owners (or even the owners before them) had a pipe burst in their master bathroom? Assuming they had the issue professionally repaired, it may not be visible to your nor the home inspector's naked eye. However, you need that inspector to not only identify but also determine and document that there are no hidden damages from the earlier issue that could arise and could cost your clients, as new owners, more money than they anticipated or budgeted for. So how do you protect your clients from unforeseen prior claims trouble? Order a C.L.U.E® report.

Get a C.L.U.E.®

When shopping for used cars, buyers will request a CARFAX® report to learn any history of accident or flood damage. Sellers may provide the CARFAX® report to prospective buyers to alleviate their fears of buying a used car.

When financing a large purchase, lenders will pull a credit reports to get a better look at the borrowers' financial history.

History matters.

When you are representing buyers or sellers of a property, request a C.L.U.E® report. The Comprehensive Loss Underwriting Exchange (C.L.U.E®) is a database of claims history on millions of homes. An overwhelming majority of insurers provide claims data to the database. The C.L.U.E® report will show up to the previous seven years of claims history on a particular address. As a real estate agent, suggest a C.L.U.E.® report be ordered by the owner as early as possible. Such advice benefits both sellers and buyers.

When representing sellers, advise them to order the C.L.U.E.® report as you take the listing. Assuming they have not ordered one in the last 12 months, it should be free. The report can be ordered by having the owner call LexisNexis® at 1-866-312-8076.

If they are required to pay, the cost is minimal. Having a C.L.U.E.® report prior to receiving offers allows for three advantages:

1. The sellers have time to dispute any inaccuracies found in the report. Unfortunately, without an early report, a contract would likely have to fall out due to insurance being too expensive or denied based on a falsehood prior to the inaccuracy being discovered. No real estate agent wants to see that happen.

2. The sellers have another item to prove they worked towards full disclosure, and it should be referenced in their sellers' disclosure. They have chosen to deliver the report, thus disclose its contents. By asking for the report to be provided to buyers, you, their listing agent, may have also lessened your disclosure liability.

3. Should the sellers receive a clean report, potential buyers are likely to receive it as a peace of mind that moving forward with the home is a sensible decision. Should the report have past claims, the buyers will have it in time to alert the home inspector so it can be documented that proper repairs were made and

that no additional issues should result. The home inspection findings can then be presented to insurers if need be. An early report has the potential of getting buyers to closing who may have otherwise had to cancel the contract.

When representing buyers, ask the listing agent for the C.L.U.E.® report when you know your clients are serious about making an offer on the property. An insurance contingency in your offer is recommended, but getting the report prior to the home inspection allows the buyers to have the inspector pay close attention to any areas of repairs indicated on the claims history. A report with multiple claims would trigger you as an agent to make certain your buyers are immediately seeking multiple bids to find a reasonable insurance premium for the property. Your request for the report will provide more answers for your buyers to make an informed decision about their purchase, and it will make you a hero for "having their back." You have now given them an opportunity to uncover potential landmines, and they will likely feel better moving forward. The insurance companies use these reports to judge whether or not a risk is worth insuring. Your clients will appreciate having the same opportunity!

What's the Deal with Deductibles?

One of the most important parts of the homeowners insurance policy is the deductible. As mentioned previously, the insurance companies offer various deductible options, and there can be a significant effect on the premium depending on how high of a deductible is selected.

The rule of thumb is that owners should choose the highest deductible they can afford in the event of a claim issue. If the options are $500 or $2,500, the owners have to decide whether they would have the funds available to cover the higher deductible. While choosing the higher deductible does result in a lower premium, it may not be a prudent decision if the insured would not have the funds available in the event they are needed to pay the deductible. Homeowners insurance is designed for catastrophic events, not for the everyday issues that help maintain a property.

A Flood of Questions

An important part of making sure your clients' home is protected involves flood insurance. Flood insurance is a misunderstood product. As such, this policy is typically overlooked, and buyers often take the stance that, "I don't need flood insurance. I've never had a flood issue." or, "This is not a high risk flood location." The home being located in a flood zone is not the sole criteria as to whether one should purchase flood insurance. Flood is defined as a temporary condition where two or more acres of normally dry land or two or more properties are inundated by water or mudflow. Just because an area has not experienced a flood in the past does not mean it won't in the future. Many conditions can lead to a flood:

- Dams
- Heavy rain
- Ice melting
- New development
- Tropical storms and hurricanes
- Winter rainy season
- Overtopped levees
- Mudflows
- Outdated or clogged drainage systems

According to the National Flood Insurance Program (NFIP), all 50 states have experienced floods in the past 5 years. Just a few inches of water can cause tens of thousands of dollars in damage. The best course of action is to deal with an experienced agent who can help you determine what steps to take to make sure your clients have all the information they need to make the best decision. If the property is determined to be in a flood risk area, then a flood elevation certificate will need to be obtained. This may already exist with the current owner, or it may need to be obtained through the county building department. Once flood zone of the property is determined, the insurance agent can quote different options. The policy quote will include coverage for the dwelling and for the contents. If a mortgage is involved, flood insurance will be a requirement if the property is in a high risk zone. Even buyers in low risk areas should consider purchasing flood insurance since a good percentage of floods occur in low risk areas. For example, it is not uncommon for the construction of new developments in an area, with no past history of flooding, to alter topography and increase the flood risk for existing homes.

Note that flood insurance is not only for homeowners, but can be purchased by renters and condo unit owners. Remember to try to obtain your quotes before your Inspection Period ends. Better safe than sorry.

To Replace or Not To Replace

As mentioned previously, your clients' homeowners insurance coverage is based on replacement value. Replacement value is not the same thing as market value. For the owner occupied, single family home (HO-3), replacement means covering for the cost to rebuild.

Probably the most common questions or discussions had between an insurance agent and their clients regarding home insurance has to do with their policy coverage (replacement) amount. Once again, the purpose of the homeowners insurance is to rebuild or replace the home to its condition prior to the peril event. During different housing market conditions, it could cost more or less to rebuild a home then it would sell for in the market.

The last thing the homeowners would want is for the home to be destroyed and the payment from the insurance company be insufficient to rebuild the home. For example, let's say you have a client, Joe Schmoe. He is looking to save money wherever he can, starting with the homeowners insurance. He decides on a 1,900 square foot, 25-year-old, 3 bedroom home with a pool, tile roof, and 2 ½ baths. Joe tells his insurance agent, "Just cover the home for $150,000. I don't need any more coverage than that." His longtime agent obliges, not wanting to lose Joe's business. Six months later, a fire destroys Joe's home. After meeting with contractors and his builder, Joe finds out that the estimated cost to rebuild his home is almost $200,000. Because of his policy limits, he will have to pay the additional $50,000 out of his pocket. Joe's agent failed him by not explaining that this exact scenario could result if he followed Joe's directive.

In a period of inflated housing prices, you may come across a home that is worth more in the open market than it would cost to replace.

The insurance agent must work with the insurance company during the initial quoting process to come up with a replacement cost estimation. This may be more or less than the property market value, depending on market conditions. However, it will give the best idea of what the rebuilding cost is so your clients can make sure that their coverage keeps up with building costs and inflation year after year. They don't want to meet Joe Schmoe's fate.

Does the Association Cover That?

One of the most common types of insurance policies in coastal and retirement areas is the Condo/Townhome unit policy (HO-6). Insurance agents who provide insurance for condo/townhome dwellers know that explaining and selling the proper coverages can be quite a challenge.

The first major hurdle is to convince the prospective unit owners that they need to purchase any property coverage at all. Too many unit owners are under the mistaken idea that the association insurance is all encompassing. "My association fees include insurance, so I don't have to buy any on my own." That notion is inaccurate from both a home-owners coverage perspective as well as a flood insurance coverage perspective. As we discussed earlier, HO-6 policies cover inside the unit, past the drywall, and the unit owners contents as well. The association master policy is a policy intended for the exterior of the building and what is behind its interior walls of each unit.

Unit owners need to select a limit of insurance based on the items that are their insurance responsibility. Some of the items that unit owners are responsible for include:

- Floor coverings, wall coverings, and ceiling coverings (paint, wallpaper, etc.)
- Electrical fixtures
- Appliances
- Air conditioning or heating equipment

- Water heaters
- Water filters
- Built in cabinets and counter tops
- Window treatments, including curtains, drapes, blinds, and hardware

If any of those items mentioned above have been upgraded, the coverage limits would need to be reviewed so that adequate coverage is offered. Besides coverage for the structural items of the unit, the owners will also want to cover their personal property (contents). This typically includes anything that can be taken out of the unit. Remember, "If you were to turn the unit upside down, whatever falls out is personal property." This limit of coverage would best be chosen by the unit buyers, because they would know better than anyone the value and quantity of their personal property.

The last part of the HO-6 policy is the personal liability/medical payments. As mentioned previously from other policy types, this is coverage to protect against the amount that the owners are liable for in the event that someone is injured on the property. Although higher and lower options can be found, the most common option limit for coverage is $300,000.

In coastal areas, windstorm coverage would be offered to protect against damage within the unit resulting from a hurricane or tropical event.

It's a Dog Eat Dog World

Pets in the home are becoming increasing more common. If your clients have pets, especially a dog, the insurance agent must be told at the time of quote so a carrier that is willing to provide coverage can be found. According to the Insurance Information Institute (III), claims as a result of dog bites (and other dog related injuries) accounted for one-third of all monies paid out in 2014. Moreover, the national average for a dog bite claim pay out was $32,072. Over $530 million dollars were paid out by insurance companies in 2014 as a result of dog related injuries.* It is no wonder that many insurance companies have excluded animal liability completely from their homeowners insurance policies. However, there are some companies that will allow an endorsement to be purchased that will cover animal liability. There are also specialty insurance companies that offer canine liability policies or general animal liability. This can be a good piece of mind for pet owners, considering it may only be a matter of "when" not "if" they suffer an animal liability claim. Talk to an agent about what might be best for your specific client.

One carrier may deny coverage due to a specific breed where as another may offer coverage. Common breeds of concern are:

- Pit Bulls and Staffordshire Terriers
- Doberman Pinschers
- Rottweilers
- German Shepherds

You may come across a situation where your clients have a dog but do not wish to disclose it to their insurance agent for fear of getting their homeowners insurance policy cancelled. I have seen situations where an insurance inspector, who is hired to do a routine inspection for the insurance company, reports a dog barking and alerts the agent. This will prompt the insurance company to request information about the dog (age, breed, and bite history). If this information is not provided, the policy will be cancelled. So it's always best to disclose, otherwise you run the risk of committing insurance fraud. Don't forget, if that dog does bite and there is not insurance coverage, the resulting bills, fines, and/or awards will have to be paid out of pocket by owner.

Landlord Beware

If you have clients who are looking to buy an investment property to rent, do not fail to press upon them that they should have homeowners

---

* "Dog Bites Accounted For More Than One-Third Of All Homeowners Liability Pay Outs Last Year As Cost Per Claim Soars." *III.* Insurance Information Institute, 13 May 2015. Web. 14 Sept. 2016.

insurance for that property as well. Sometimes, if buyers are not financing the property purchase and therefore do not have a lender requiring the property to be insured, they wrongly assume if it's not required it must be superfluous.

Having insurance, or not having insurance, does not decrease or increase the likelihood of something happening on or to the property. It only determines whether or not the owners will have to shoulder the entire cost when something does happen.

The Dwelling Policy (DP), as mentioned previously, is the best option for future landlords. The buyers can get a policy that will cover the building and liability. They have the option to cover personal property contents. However, in most cases landlords do not have personal property in a leased home.

Too many landlords fail to require tenants who are renting the property to purchase a HO-4 (renters) policy for their own personal items. Let's say Jill is renting a home from Jack. In the unfortunate event that a fire breaks out and destroys the building, Jack would be covered by his DP to replace and/or rebuild the home. If Jill had purchased a HO-4 policy, her contents would be replaced up to the policy limits. Due to the unforeseen nature of these types of events, it is wise for you to encourage landlords to recommend or even require that their tenants purchase a HO-4 policy. If landlords wish to make the tenants acquire a HO-4 policy, this stipulation should be disclosed during negotiations as it places an additional cost on the tenants. Once agreed upon, it should be clearly spelled out in the lease, stating, "Tenants agree to acquire renter's insurance with a minimum of $____ of coverage by the lease commencement date, and will keep the policy in force through lease term. Landlords' names (or corporate entity name that the property is owned under) shall be named as additional insured on the policy."

Clients' Homeowners Insurance Quotes

Once your buyers find a home they are sincerely considering making an offer on, it is time to look at pricing a home insurance policy.

What information does an insurance agent need to provide your clients with the best quote? Obviously, the more information you can give to the agent, the better. The following are the essential items that an agent will require:

1. Property address
2. Age of home
3. Construction type
4. Type and age of roof
5. Other structures (carport, fence, pool, screen enclosure, etc.)
6. Buyers' names and contact information

Additionally, if you have former reports or are further along than the offer stage in the home-buying process, the insurance agent's ability to quote a policy would benefit by being provided:

7. Home Inspection
8. Appraisal
9. Wind Mitigation report (coastal areas)

An experienced, knowledgeable agent should have multiple choices of insurance companies, and will use all of the information gathered to secure the best possible quote options.

Who's Liable for That?

One of the most overlooked portions of a home insurance policy is the Personal Liability. Your clients may have concerns about how to be protected in the event of an unforeseen accident injuring another person. What if a neighbor is bitten by a dog? What if a tree falls from their yard onto the next door neighbors' fence? What if someone slips and falls on the front side walk?

The liability section of the policy covers bodily injury and property damage suffered in connection with the property. Medical payments for others is also part of this coverage. The typical homeowners insurance policy offers at least $100,000 in liability coverage "per occurrence," but most policies offer up to $300,000. It protects you against many types of accidents and occurrences, including slip-and-fall injuries on your property and dog bites to the letter carrier. Simply put, if the homeowners, or a family member living in the home, are found responsible for someone else's bodily injury or property damage, the personal liability coverage should step in and pay the damages. Some insurance policies will also pay to defend their clients if they are named in a lawsuit. This does not cover intentional injuries, only negligence.

The liability part of the homeowners insurance covers both at home and away. Away addresses accidents that are caused by the homeowners or their family that lives with them, even away from the home. An example would include damage done to your neighbor's siding by your son's baseball. General exceptions to the away portion of coverage include claims resulting from:

- Accidents covered by auto insurance policies
- Business related events
- Intentional acts
- Accidents covered by worker's compensation claims

Medical expenses incurred due to someone being injured on the property are also covered. This does not include the homeowners or residents living in the home. Medical expenses may include reasonable charges for medical, surgical, X-ray, dental, ambulance, hospital, and professional nursing services, as well as prosthetic devices and funeral services.

Expenses from a lawsuit can add up, so when your clients are reviewing their policy, they should make sure to choose the highest liability option offered by the insurance company. In most cases, there is no more than a $20-$30 addition to the premium.

Umbrella Policy, Because When it Rains it Pours

If your clients are inclined to have lots of guests at their home, or they like to throw parties, they may wish to consider an umbrella liability policy. This coverage is in excess of the standard coverage offered through the home insurance policy. In most cases, it is a separate policy altogether. However, it can be well worth the extra expense. An umbrella liability policy would kick in after the underlying home or auto liability policies are exhausted. For example, home owner Bob is found liable in a $500,000 lawsuit for an injury suffered by a guest at his property. Typically, the homeowners insurance would cover up to the limit (most commonly $300,000), and the umbrella policy would come in for the rest of the damage.

Without adequate protection, a large judgement against the homeowners could cost them their assets, as well as future potential earnings and inheritances. An umbrella policy for one million dollars can cost as low as $250 annually. It also takes into account vehicles, watercraft, and other possessions to determine the rates. The insurance agent can go over the options and what the best course of action for your clients is. In some cases, this can mean bundling auto and home insurance together to get the best umbrella rate.

According to the Insurance Information Institute (III), some of the most common liability insurance claims for homeowners are:

- **Dog Bites** – as mentioned previously, a typical homeowners insurance policy includes liability coverage for damages and injuries caused by the homeowners or other members of the household, including pets. Insurers often exclude some dog breeds from their policies because they represent higher risks. Dog breeds frequently excluded by carriers include pit bulls, Akitas and German shepherds. If insurance companies determine that a dog breed is dangerous, it can be more costly for the owners to find home coverage. The excluded dogs usually are large and powerful breeds that can cause serious injuries if they attack people.

- **Home Accidents** – While most home accidents do not involve liability claims, they are still fairly common. Even if someone comes to the property uninvited, like a salesperson, the homeowners can be held liable for any injuries they sustain if they are found negligent. Another example would be a visitor tripping on a piece of loose carpet or flooring, or a visitor who fell because of a loose stairway railing. (These are items that could be discovered during the home inspection.)

- **Falling trees** – during a wind, snow, or ice storm, falling trees are a common hazard. If homeowners have a tree on their property that falls and damages a neighbor's property, they can be held liable. In the event that a tree falls on a neighbor's car, it can be a significant cost to replace the vehicle. Insurance companies try to prevent this by requiring homeowners to trim any branches that may pose a hazard, either to the home or to neighboring property.

- **Intoxicated Guests** – If the homeowners frequently like to host parties and a guest becomes intoxicated and does harm to a person or property, the host can be liable. Care should always be taken in this situation.

- **Injury to domestic workers** – Such workers include home cleaners, lawn maintenance, or pool cleaners, all of whom could sustain an injury while working on the property. The homeowners may be liable for damages.

Rate vs. Premium

Often, the terms "rate" and "premium" are used interchangeably when talking about insurance. An explanation of the difference can be found in the formula: rate X exposure units = premium. Rate is the cost of insurance per exposure to cover claims payments, expenses, and commissions to agents (assuming an agent is used) and provide for a reasonable profit. Replacing a house can depend on a variety of factors, such as its location, size of the home, type of construction, and changes in building codes, all which would be factored into the rate. The rate is a number that an insurance company sets as its price, much in the same way a gas station sets its cost per gallon. Exposure Unit refers to the item exposed to loss that is insured by the insurance company. For example, the exposure unit in homeowners insurance can be expressed in terms of what it costs to replace a house if it is destroyed. Premium is what you pay as a result of the rate multiplied by the number of exposure units you insure. It is the amount you write the check for once a month, yearly, etc.

For example, if the rate per $1,000 of coverage is $10.00 per year, and you have a home that would be replaced for $200,000 if destroyed, then the annual premium would be $2,000. Since there are a number of factors, fees and charges that can make up the bottom line premium, the buyer should discuss any questions with the insurance agent.

From Trash to Treasure

So your clients have found their dream home. However, it is actually a nightmare. It was previously a foreclosure, but they intend to fix it up and make it their gem. It is a common scenario, but this can make getting homeowners insurance a challenge. Most homebuyers don't think much about the process of getting insurance. They believe it's just part of the buying process. They will get quotes, pay for their first year's premiums at closing, and roll their payments into escrow. Pretty simple, right?

Sometimes it is this simple getting insurance on a fixer-upper, but more often than not your buyers may have to do some more shopping around. Fixer-upper homes – especially those that have been foreclosed on or abandoned – are a higher risk for insurance companies. The fixing up process itself comes with some risks, including problems that might occur when no one is living in the home during the renovation process.

Since more issues could arise, fewer insurers are willing to take on the risk. Those that are willing to insure these properties will charge more for homeowners insurance. Luckily, there are some options for getting insurance on fixer-uppers, even if it's in terrible condition:

1. **Conventional Insurance** – If the home simply needs some basic repairs, and your clients will be able to complete repairs and move in within 30 days of closing, they can likely get a conventional insurance policy through a traditional insurance company.

   But what if the home is in really bad shape? What if they won't move into it for months? Even if they do move in quickly, what if some of the major repairs (like exterior siding and/or gutter repairs) will take a few months to complete?

In this case, the traditional insurance company will likely recommend another type of insurance, specifically formulated for
higher-risk situations like that. (Empty and under-construction
homes are particularly high risk for insurance companies.)

2. **Builder's Risk** – This is the most common type of renovation
   or new construction homeowners insurance. Builder's risk policies are easiest to get if there is a solid, timely plan to finish the
   reconstruction. The agent can quote and customize the policy
   for the specific situation.

3. **Vacant Dwelling** – If the home needs cosmetic work, and will
   not be occupied during the renovations, a vacant dwelling policy would be possible. This type of policy will protect against
   physical loss, but usually does not cover theft. This may or may
   not be a problem depending on where the home is located and
   if the home contains valuable appliances or tools.

More about Binders

You have been working with your clients for several weeks (or months
depending on the situation), trying to find the best home for them.
There has been good and bad, but now they have finally decided. They
have notified their mortgage lender to proceed, and they've been in-
structed to get a "binder" from their insurance agent. As mentioned
earlier, this is basically the insurance company saying that the property
meets their underwriting guidelines (from the information they have
gathered so far), and they are ready to proceed with issuing a policy.
The binder period is typically 30 days, and this will show the mortgage
company that there is an active policy in effect to cover the home at
closing. With most mortgage transactions, the insurance premium for
the first year will be collected as part of the closing costs. The mortgage
company will be responsible to pay for the renewal insurance each year
after from the borrowers' escrow account. If this is not the way the
mortgage company has set up the loan, then the homeowners will be
required to make the insurance payment soon after the binder is issued
(typically 10-15 days). Most insurance companies offer a payment plan
to allow the premium payment to be spread out quarterly or semiannu-
ally. Some will also offer premium financing, which allow payments on

a monthly basis, but will charge interest (sometimes running as high as 25%). Nearly all will allow for credit cards to be used for payment as well.

What happens if the new buyers make a premium payment to secure the binder, and the property purchase falls through? In this case, all they have to do is to notify their insurance agent, and the policy will be cancelled. A full premium refund will be issued back to the policyholder.

In some cases, a policy is cancelled within a few months of the binder being issued. This would most likely be done by the insurance company if they find something about the property or the homeowners that was not known/disclosed at the time of binding. This may include:

- Vicious dog (or animal)
- Home in poor condition
- Insured with multiple undisclosed claims
- Previous fraudulent insurance activity

If the issue would cause the home to not meet the insurance company underwriting guidelines, then a cancellation notice will be issued, giving the homeowners 30-45 days to find a replacement policy. Any premiums paid would be prorated and refunded back the insured.

There are cases where an issue can be explained and the policy can remain active. For example, let's say the buyers have purchased an older home with a pool. It may be that the previous owners did not keep up with the maintenance, or maybe the pool is empty. The insurance companies DO NOT like to see empty pools, as these can be a potentially large liability issue if someone were to fall in. The homeowners can typically repair and fill the pool, providing pictures to the insurance company, who will then likely reinstate any policies affected by a cancellation notice. Alternatively, it could be that there is damage to the soffit areas of the roof, and there are trees overhanging the property. Proof of repairs and pictures showing the trimming is all that would be needed in most cases to keep the policy active. This is another example showing how important having a good insurance agent can be. If these items are not addressed, the insurance company will simply cancel the policy, and the owner will be left with no coverage. Having an agent who represents a wide range of insurance companies will help to solve the problem as quickly as possible. I cannot tell you how many times I have had to work with clients to get their policy reviewed for reinstatement after it was discovered the home had one or more issues (i.e. a broken or boarded window, peeling paint on the exterior of the home, missing or damaged roof shingles, or a screen patio missing screen panels). Having an agent with the knowledge and relationships with the insurance companies can take the headache out of running the risk of being uninsured.

PROTECT YOURSELF

One of the most overlooked tools that a real estate agent can have is insurance. There are various types of insurance to consider, ranging from fire and property coverage to automobile insurance, and of course error and omissions insurance.

To Err is Human

One area of coverage that is probably the most important for a real estate agent to have is error and omissions insurance (E&O). Face it; we live in a litigious society. Turn on the TV during any period of the day, and you'll hear five different commercials for attorneys looking to "get the most money" for their clients. Do not practice real estate without an E&O policy to protect you.

Basically, E&O insurance provides coverage for situations where a real estate professional has failed to carry out their professional responsibilities or has been found negligent. Unfortunately, different insurance companies' E&O policy terms can vary from one to another. *Always read your policy* to know specifically what it does and does not cover. If your broker provides the E&O insurance for the associates, ask for a copy. Similar to a homeowners insurance policy, there are several parts or terms of the policy to consider:

- What is covered?
- Who is covered?
- Policy conditions and limitations
- Costs and deductibles

If you are a broker, you will want to know if the policy will cover employees, assistants, and/or agents. For an agent, typically, the "named insured" is the person who obtains the policy. You want to make sure that the policy covers all aspects of the real estate business that you will be involved in. If you find exclusions in the policy that are vital to your business, make sure you request coverage. Exclusions can be as common as no criminal acts by the insured, failing to disclose issues related to the property, or discrimination. They can also be more involved, such as related business activities like property management, violations of laws, or dealing with properties owned by the E&O insured. Read the policy!

As mentioned, make sure that the policy provides coverage to fit the way you operate your business. For example, if you use lock boxes, make sure the policy includes incidents related to using lock boxes. Residential and commercial transactions differ in their complexities, so make sure the policy is designed for one and/or the other. For an additional premium, most insurance carriers will allow you to add exclusions back into the policy on case-by-case basis. You will also want to understand the effective date and when coverage begins and ends. Most policies are issued on either a "claims made" basis or "occurrence." A claims made policy covers only claims that are filed during the term of the policy and for a short time after expiration. An occurrence policy will cover claims made for events that occurred before or after the policy effective dates, depending on the specifics of the policy. The dollar limits for the policy must be appropriate for the business risk. The limit is the maximum amount of coverage available for an individual claim. There is a "per claim" limit and an "aggregate" limit. Read how and when notice of claims or potential claims must be given. Do not hesitate to ask your broker's insurance agent questions about the policy and its coverage.

Taxi!

As you are growing your business and expanding your territory, you will spend a lot of time driving your car. When possible, drive separately from your clients, both for liability and physical safety's sake. As driving clients can never be fully avoided in your line of work, make sure you've researched your auto coverage and have secured the appropriate policy. Does your personal auto policy cover your business driving? Most likely, yes. While most personal auto policies do not cover for "business use," many personal auto policies (PAP) include provisions designed for agents or others with similar business, which consists of coverage for driving for work and with clients. If you uncover any gaps in your PAP, you may need to get a commercial auto policy. Also, if you own a real estate agency and have registered vehicles in the name of the business, you will need a commercial policy. Note that some brokerages will require their agents to name the realty office as an Additional Insured on their PAP. This can usually be accomplished with a quick phone call to your insurance agent and at no cost to you.

General Liability Insurance

General liability coverage (GL) can be an important tool for a brokerage and/or agent to have. However, it should not be confused with professional liability insurance, which is the agent E&O policy. While the E&O policy covers issues related to the real estate transaction with a client, the GL protects against legal action taken as a result of something more general in nature. It could be as simple as a client or associate who is hurt at your office or bodily injury alleged at any location where business is done. One million dollars is the most common coverage limit, although policy limits can very. This policy can be combined with property coverage as part of a business owners policy (BOP). Physical loss to any type of business property, such as office equipment, can be included. The BOP is most often issued as a package to include both types of coverage. How much coverage you'll need will depend on various factors, such as location and type of risk that you face in your real estate business. The policy can be tailored to your needs, and includes coverage for legal fees and even defamation and copyright infringement. Talk to your agent about what coverage best suits your needs.

Umbrella

There are many different types of insurance, and while not all policies are necessary for everyone, some are commonly overlooked. One such type of coverage is an Umbrella policy. The purpose of this type of policy is to offer coverage "in excess" of the underlying limits on your other policies. An umbrella policy is an extra layer of coverage to protect against the unexpected scenario. If a client is injured on your business premises, or while you are showing them property, you could be liable for damages. While other liability policies may be exhausted (general liability, personal homeowners), an umbrella policy would offer coverage above those limits. For example, let's say a client trips and falls on a property you are showing to them and the judgement is two million dollars. Your general liability with a one million dollar limit will cover part of the claim, while a one million dollar umbrella policy, if you have one, could cover the rest. Keep in mind that it does not offer coverage without the other policy; it cannot stand alone. It is solely coverage above and beyond other policies. Talk to your agent to learn if an umbrella policy is right for your situation.

BUSINESS
LAW

Dear Real Estate Agent,

Being a business attorney has many facets beyond just knowing law; being a real estate agent encompasses much more than just knowing how to pen a sale. Neither of us can be successful in our professions without becoming proficient in running a business, which includes accounting, marketing, client acquisition, human resources, and management. We are similar.

Your industry is somewhat unique in the fact that most of you are independent contractors, and thus independent business owners. I'm unsure how much this resonates with the average agent. I know many agents work diligently to protect their clients. However, I watch many of those same agents fail to protect themselves business-wise. That said, a strong agent will learn not only all the legalities of real estate as it impacts their clients but also *those laws that impact the agents themselves, from a business owner standpoint.*

Be wise, determine what needs to be known about the law with respect to your business. It will both protect you and set you apart. I encourage you to befriend a business attorney, create a business relationship with a real estate lawyer, and attend classes to keep your legal knowledge up to date. The successful agents I know tend to be lifelong learners.

Being a real estate agent is a good career choice; becoming a successful agent is a rewarding choice.

Sincerely,

Kelly Sturmthal, Esq.
DSM LAW/Sturmthal & Associates, PA

BUSINESS LAW FOR REAL ESTATE AGENTS

As an agent, you are more likely than not an independent contractor. Knowing what that means is essential, as it defines your relationship with your broker and strongly shapes your working agreement with one another.

INDEPENDENT CONTRACTOR DEFINED

The legal definition of an independent contractor is a person who contracts to do work for another person according to his or her own processes and methods; the contractor is not subject to another's control except for what is specified in a mutually binding agreement for a specific job.

If you are an independent contractor, *you are self-employed*. If what you are doing or how you are doing it is controlled by an employer, you are *not* an independent contractor. This applies even if you are given freedom of action. If the employer has the legal right to control the details of how the services are performed, then you are not an independent contractor.

The independent contractor status largely serves to establish to the IRS that you are not an employee of the company. As an Independent Contractor, you have certain tax obligations that are outlined at IRS.gov. Review the IRS.gov information so that you are informed. *If the IRS decides that the relationship is that of an employee/employer instead of an independent contractor, both parties may be subject to additional taxes and penalties such as re-filing, back taxes for employer, and elimination of the option to deduct business expenses.*

INDEPENDENT CONTRACTOR AGREEMENT WITH BROKER

"Must Have" Clauses

When you are signing a contract with a real estate broker as an independent contractor (known as "IC"), the contract must clearly state that your status is that of an independent contractor. Here are several statements (or similar wording or clauses) that must be part of your contract:

1. IC will be construed as an agent.

2. IC will not be deemed a servant, employee, or partner of Broker for any purpose.

3. IC will not be treated as an employee for federal tax purposes.

4. IC is responsible for paying her/his own estimated income tax payments, self-employment taxes, occupational taxes, and other taxes, if any, to the appropriate governmental entities.

5. Broker will not withhold any taxes from compensation due to IC.

6. Broker will not provide workers compensation insurance for IC.

Service contracts may utilize the word "associate" instead of the above "IC."

Additional Clauses to Establish Independent Contractor Status

A contract may also include additional conditions that establish you as an independent contractor. For example:

1. **Benefits** – Independent Contractor is not eligible for and has no claim to medical benefits, profit sharing, vacation pay, sick pay, or other benefits offered to employees.

2. **Expenses** – Independent Contractor is responsible for expenses and materials necessary to perform services required in Scope of Work. (If you anticipate large expenses, such as travel or expensive software, you should factor these into your commission negotiations and make sure you make enough to cover them. However, if you meet most other independent contractor status conditions, you could stipulate that the client will reimburse you for certain large expenses.)

General Agreement Understanding

Your agreement is binding, and it should be read carefully. A good contract for an agent has a "give and take" for both parties signing the agreement. Closely read the clauses that address the following so that you understand your responsibilities under the contract, *before signing*:

1. When does the contract begin and end?

2. Does the agreement state the term of the working relationship? Make sure the length of the term is reasonable so that it does not imply an employee relationship.

3. Under what circumstances can either party terminate the contract before the end date and what, if any, obligations does the terminating party owe to the other party?

4. Specify that either party can terminate the agreement for business-related reasons with a minimum 30-day period of notice to avoid looking like an employee.

The following points should be included in any standard contract and especially your services agreement.

1. Identification of parties; signatures of these parties
2. Agreed upon statements
3. Term of contract
4. Default and Remedies
5. Applicable state law
6. Confidentiality
7. Notices

COLLABORATION AGREEMENTS FOR TEAMS

Teams are becoming increasingly common in the real estate industry. As more agents find themselves joining or creating a team, agreements outlining these new relationships need to be understood. Collaborations formed for business purposes should *always* be approved by the broker and be solidified by *signing a written agreement* with all parties. The agreement should at minimum address the following:

- **Who** pays for what?

- **What** happens if the agreement is terminated in regard to clients that had been acquired through joint marketing and advertising efforts? How will commissions derived from servicing those clients be distributed moving forward?

- **Why** are you collaborating? What skills and commitments are each of you bringing to the team?

- **When** does the relationship terminate?

- **How** do you handle the exceptions? Are there any services, for example rentals, that only one of the parties will perform? If so, will they receive more or all of commissions derived from such performance? Are there former clients of any party that must be excluded from the new partnership? If so, are the names of those clients listed on the agreement itself?

This collaboration contract legally binds those that sign it. If you believe your business relationship warrants clauses that haven't been addressed, add them to the agreement. Obviously, you must avoid any terms that may not be legally enforceable (i.e. excessive fees).

A word of caution, business partnerships are often entered into too early and too lightly. It's usually a happy, exciting time when new partnerships form. However, all too often, partners fail to live up to one another's expectations. Personalities clash, different work styles prove cumbersome, etc. The reasons partnerships need to rewrite agreements or terminate altogether are long and varied. As such, I strongly suggest either initially drafting the agreement for a short trial period or including a clause that allows for the terms of the agreement to be revisited within three to six months. Hope for the best, but prepare for the worst. Moreover, always get a legal review of your contract for peace of mind.

REAL ESTATE LIABILITY AND CORPORATE PROTECTIONS

Protect you *and* your business. From the legal standpoint, one of the goals of any professional should include protecting what you are building as your business.

Too many real estate professionals solely rely on an errors and omissions insurance policy to protect them, yet this protection has limitations. Without a corporate protection, if your insurance limit is too low to cover a claim, the injured party can go after your business *and personal* assets for the difference.

Legal Structure. The four main options are as follows. *Note: each state has specific established rules for the various structures. Moreover, some may only be allowed for brokerages, not individual real estate agents. Check with your state licensing department before forming any entity.*

1. Run your business as an individual sole proprietor.

2. Create a general partnership or limited liability partnership.

3. Incorporate as a C-corporation (potentially filing as a sub chapter S corp.).

4. Structure your business as a limited liability company, also known as a LLC.

Sole Proprietor – If you work as a sole proprietor, you will be held personally responsible for all debts and lawsuits incurred by the business. This option does not offer any asset protection. In other words, *if the business is sued, all of your personal assets are at risk.*

General or Limited Liability Partnership – General partnership structures create a liability situation even if you are not at fault. Both parties of a partnership are liable, completely. There are limited liability partnerships that allow owners to limit their liability. Typically, the limited liability also includes limited management authority.

Partnerships are viable if you have the right partner. Take the time to get to know your partner's business and personal philosophy with respect to fairness, financial issues, and personnel issues prior to entering into any partnership.

C Corporation, with a sub chapter S corporation IRS filing – An S Corporation is a standard C Corporation that has elected a special tax status with the IRS. The S Corporation requirements are generally the same as those for C Corporations. The S Corporation's special tax status eliminates the double-taxation that can occur with a C Corporation's income. A corporate income tax return is filed, but tax is NOT paid at the corporate level. Instead, business profits or losses "pass-through" to shareholders and are then reported on their individual tax returns. Any tax due is paid by shareholders at their individual tax rates.

Professional Association (PA) – The PA is a legal entity formed to provide professional services. States may dictate which services are allowed to form Professional Associations, and typically those who form the association must be licensed with the state for their profession. A Professional Association is similar to a corporation in how it is formed and protects the professional from personal liability.

Limited Liability Corporation (LLC) – Although fairly new, the LLC is currently the most common legal structure for real estate agents. LLCs do not have restrictions on the number of members allowed. Check if your state license and regulation agency allows agents to form multi-member LLCs. Verify the liability protection of a single member LLC in your state. The members also have flexibility in structuring the management of the company. Florida LLCs provide members with options for the distribution of profits. It should be noted, unlike older corporate structures, there is not much LLC case law available and each state varies in its LLC structure. Therefore, it is important to keep up to date of any changes. Keep in mind, the initial and ongoing fees of an LLC are more expensive than the other legal structures. Check you state's Division of Corporations website for fees.

A more in depth look at an LLC in Florida follows (make certain to research your state's LLC regulations):

This entity may include an unlimited amount of members. An owner is referred to as a member in an LLC.

Tax benefit:

- Similar to an S-Corp, the member reports his or her share of the LLC's profit or loss on their individual tax returns if they have elected the S-Corp SS-4 status through the IRS. A Multi-member LLC may file as a general partnership, or if they file a SS-4 IRS form for a sub chapter S filing, all income or loss is filed on a Schedule C.

- Conferring with an accountant for your best option is strongly suggested.

Corporate Requirements – Unlike a C-Corp, a LLC does not require corporate minutes or resolutions but creating an Operating Agreement, a business plan, and a vision and mission statement always proves worth your time.

Operating Agreement – Although not required by Florida law, it is prudent for members of a multi-member LLC to create an operating agreement to address the particulars of the business. Members' ownership shares, rights, obligations, duties, titles, and procedures for ownership buy-outs and dissolution of the LLC should all be outlined within the agreement.

BUSINESS AND PERSONAL SAFEGUARDS WORK TOGETHER

For most of you, the number one reason to protect your business is to protect a source of income for your loved ones. As such, you will want to make certain your legal affairs regarding your personal assets are in order through a business plan, an estate plan, and a business succession plan.

Protect Your Business / Protect Your Loved Ones Checklist

____ Determine the best legal entity under which to structure your business

____ Review beneficiary designations on all bank, financial, retirement accounts, insurance policies

____ Review personal and business insurance needs

____ Make or update your Last Will and Testament and Durable Power of Attorney

____ Organize all financial and legal information in one place

____ Review contracts or agreements that your business is currently operating under

____ Make an "In Case of Emergency" plan or checklist

____ Create a business succession plan (a plan stating what happens when you want to retire or if you are unavailable to run your business)

____ Consult with a local attorney, accountant, financial planner, and insurance agent and determine their fees so you can budget for future decisions and determine the direction that is best for your individual situation

Making sure you have addressed the concerns stated in the above list best protects you, your family, and your business.

OUR CONCLUSION, YOUR BEGINNING

THAT'S ALL THEY WROTE...

So there you have it. Our greatest challenge in writing this book was that each state and region has different laws and customs within which real estate agents practice. As such, we acknowledge some of the information will not apply to your transactions, but hope that if you are not able to use specifics, you still benefited from reading our cooperative approach to real estate and thoughts on the industry.

As a real estate agent, it is your duty to seek out knowledge and acquire the experience needed to protect and guide your clients through their real estate transactions. We believe your success will be determined by 1.) your commitment to lifelong learning and 2.) your ability to surround yourself with experts in the various real estate industry related fields to work with and learn from.

Go find your real estate lawyer, insurance broker, home inspector, mortgage broker, and business attorney. Develop relationships that allow you to feel comfortable asking questions, referring clients, and sharing business opportunities. In essence, start writing the next chapters of your business...

KATHERINE SCARIM

Katherine Scarim is the broker/owner of Island Bridge Realty, in Jupiter, Florida. Island Bridge Realty was conceived in her vision of how real estate should be. As a new agent, she struggled to find the training and support she expected and needed. Today, as a non-competing broker, she is able to dedicate her to time supporting the associates by providing the training and resources she believes necessary for real estate success.

Author of *Before You Are Licensed: 13 Steps to Jumpstart Your Future Real Estate Career,* she writes to help agents flourish and, hopefully, to leave the real estate industry a little better than she found it.

Katherine lives in Jupiter, Florida, with her amazing husband of over 20 years and their five children.

GREGORY R. COHEN, ESQUIRE

Gregory R. Cohen, Esquire was born in Pittsburgh, Pennsylvania, in 1971, studied at University of Miami (B.A., 1993); University of Miami School of Law (J.D., 1996); and was admitted to The Florida Bar, 1996. Mr. Cohen is Board Certified in Real Estate by the Florida Bar.

His areas of practice at Cohen, Norris, Wolmer, Ray, Telepman, & Cohen include: residential and commercial real estate and loan transactions, including a focus on short sales and commercial workouts, issuance of title insurance, business transactions, and development transactions. Furthermore, clients consist of sellers and purchasers of residential and commercial real estate (land, retail, office) and businesses, institutional lenders on commercial and residential loan transactions, real estate agents, title insurance underwriters regarding transactional work and claims work, builders, developers, and landlords and tenants regarding residential and commercial lease transactions.

Greg has served as former Chairman of the Real Estate Committee of the Palm Beach County Bar Association. He has lectured to various professionals involved in real estate, including surveyors, real estate agents, and other lawyers (for approved Florida Bar CLE credits).

Greg lives in Palm Beach Gardens, Florida, with his wife and their three children.

GERALD PUMPHREY

Gerald Pumphrey has been a residential loan originator since graduating Florida State University in 1992. He is currently employed as a producing sales manager for the Jupiter office of Waterstone Mortgage and resides in Jupiter Florida.

GUY HARTMAN

Guy hails from Huntsville, Alabama, where he was exposed to the construction trades from a young age. His father was a bricklayer and many of his relatives were contractors or building tradesmen of different types. Guy says he's carried a lot of bricks under the critical eye of his perfectionist father. Even carrying the darn things had to be done the right way! Now living with his beautiful wife in the also beautiful Jupiter, Florida, he spends a good percentage of his off time arranging for visits from children and grandchildren. By the way, it's true, grandchildren are much more fun than their parents.

Guy proudly served 25 years as a United States Marine. Along the way, he earned an undergraduate degree in physics and a Master's degree in aviation systems. Most of his career was spent as a pilot in the cockpit of helicopters and fixed wing aircraft. Guy is most proud of being a graduate of the Navy Test Pilot School. Post Marine Corps endeavors included airline pilot and engineering test pilot for major defense contractors.

Always knowing his heart was in the trades, Guy finally had the opportunity to start a home inspection company where he capitalizes on his unique experiences. He brings a fresh perspective to the industry and challenges the status quo at every opportunity. Just because "that's the way it has always been done" is not good enough for Guy. He enjoys the work tremendously.

A dyed in the wool do-it-yourselfer, Guy was exposed to the real estate transaction process and home inspection process while buying and selling many homes during his career. About every three years he would execute orders to a new location, sell and buy another house through a new listing and buyer's agent. He quickly learned how to spot a good real estate agent, like Katherine Scarim, the co-author of this book.

He would tear the new home apart and rebuild it, one weekend at a time, to his specifications. You learn a lot about houses through this school of hard knocks. Guy says he was taught how to test aircraft, but he learned about home inspections on his own.

Guy's home inspection process and business is a unique blend of his experiences in engineering flight test and evaluation and hands on do-it-yourself home ownership. He knows what is important and what isn't. He can quickly and knowledgeably put his home inspection findings in context for both his client and the real estate agent.

Guy welcomes the opportunity to be part of this book. He hopes his home inspection views will bring fresh perspective and a better way of doing things for the real estate agent. It's important that we work together to better support our mutual clients.

MARK SHANZ

Mark Shanz has been a 2-20 licensed insurance agent for 11 years. He is the co-owner of Seegott Shanz Insurance, an independent insurance agency in Palm City, Florida. Prior to his career in the Property & Casualty field, Mark was a Financial Advisor for 12 years.

Mark was born in New York, but is almost a native Floridian, save for the few years spent in the cold Northeast attending college. He resides in Jupiter, Florida, where he has lived for 20 years with his amazing wife and two children. He spends his time away from insurance watching sports, playing golf, and spending time with family.

KELLY C. STURMTHAL, ESQ.

Kelly C. Sturmthal, Esq. left the banking industry to pursue a law degree at the University of Miami, and after graduating, she practiced in the areas of Wills and Estate Planning, General Business, and Property Tax Appeals. Years of law practice and creating and running several other businesses, including her family's medical supply business and Step Out Strategies, a business consulting firm, allows her a unique perspective when assisting families and businesses. She specializes in the areas of Wills, Estate Planning, Probate and Business Contracts, Organization, and Succession Planning with DSM LAW.

Kelly penned her fusion of business and law as co-author of *Law Office on a Laptop: How to Set Up your Own Successful Mobile Law Practice.*

Kelly enjoys living in Jupiter, Florida, with her loving husband and two amazing sons.

Made in the USA
San Bernardino, CA
26 January 2017